From Liverpool to Los Angeles

Peter Ansorge began his career as a journalist on the staff of *Plays and Players* in 1971. His articles and reviews also appeared in the *Observer* and the *Times Educational Supplement*. His account of fringe theatre, *Disrupting the Spectacle*, appeared in 1974. He joined the BBC in 1975 where his commissions included David Hare's first film, *Licking Hitler*, and innovative series such as *Gangsters* and *Empire Road*. Since 1987 he has been responsible for commissioning drama series and serials at Channel 4. His award-winning commissions include: *A Very British Coup*, *Traffik*, *GBH*, *Lipstick on Your Collar*, *The Manageress*, *Tales of the City*, *The Camomile Lawn*, *Hearts and Minds* and *The Politician's Wife*.

At Channel 4 he has worked closely with Alan Bleasdale on *GBH*, *Jake's Progress* and *Melissa*; Paula Milne on *The Politician's Wife*, *The Fragile Heart* and *Thursday the Twelfth* (1998); and the late Dennis Potter on *Lipstick on Your Collar*, *Karaoke* and *Cold Lazarus*. He is also responsible for Channel 4's long-running soap opera, *Brookside*.

in the same series

From Liverpool to Los Angeles

On Writing for Theatre, Film and Television

Peter Ansorge

faber and faber
LONDON · BOSTON

First published in 1997
by Faber and Faber Limited
3 Queen Square London WC1N 3AU

Typeset by Faber and Faber Ltd
Printed in England by Clays Ltd, St Ives plc

© Peter Ansorge, 1997

Peter Ansorge is hereby identified as author of this
work in accordance with Section 77 of the Copyright,
Designs and Patents Act 1988

A CIP record for this book
is available from the British Library

ISBN 0-571-17912-6

10 9 8 7 6 5 4 3 2 1

For Beth

Am I right or am I right?

– Dennis Potter, *The Singing Detective*

Contents

Introduction

This is a book about changes that have taken place in theatre, film and television since the beginning of the 1980s. The writer's role in these changes is at the heart of the discussion. As a nation we are comfortable with the idea that nothing essential ever alters. Tradition and evolution govern our thinking about society in much the same way that the idea of revolution once preoccupied the French. Yet, looking at the post-war period, it is our society that has experienced far greater upheavals. By comparison, the French way of life has remained pretty stable even when taking into account the student uprisings of 1968. It is England that has constantly reinvented itself and chosen to alter the rules for each new generation. As a character in David Hare's play, *Teeth 'n' Smiles*, remarks: 'One day it's a revolution to swear on the bus. The next it's the only way to get a ticket.'

Nowhere can this be seen more clearly than in our cultural life. Twenty years ago I wrote a book about fringe playwrights entitled *Disrupting the Spectacle*. There was a great deal in it about a theatre of confrontation, attack and sometimes sheer silliness. It was a time when the young could really enjoy themselves. We were allowed to indulge in the most surreal events and still call them theatre. Students today are often taught by people whose radical politics were formed during the 1960s. If they are so inclined, they must imagine that the world of the media is packed with figures who are in active opposition to the mainstream. But they should not be fooled. Despite the arrival of a new Labour government, it is worth remembering that we have been living through a deeply conservative time in the arts, and not just in terms of party politics. The most

radical teacher at a university or the bravest current affairs producer at the BBC today will not have the same confidence in their
jobs as twenty years ago. Then the centre still held: the BBC, the
National Theatre and our major cultural institutions had not yet
experienced the cutbacks and assaults of the 1980s.

Yet, despite the cutbacks, our theatres and television companies
appear in remarkably good shape. Under Stephen Daldry the
English Stage Company has moved into the West End from the
Royal Court with all the critical trumpets sounding. Trevor Nunn
is taking over a National Theatre from Richard Eyre that is in the
very best of health. Sir Peter Hall has announced a bold season of
new plays and classic revivals at the Old Vic. Meanwhile our
broadcasters face an unparalleled era of expansion and opportunity. Quality crime drama like *Prime Suspect* and *Cracker* dominates the schedules of a confident ITV. As director-general, John
Birt has claimed that his reorganization of the BBC has led to a
new golden age of creativity ushered in by the success of its 1995
adaptation of *Pride and Prejudice*. New television channels are
announced daily to feed the voracious hunger of the coming digi-
tal age. Yet it is my contention that much of this bravura is based
on a false perception. Our drama is in fact less confident and
adventurous than twenty years ago.

The following chapters on theatre, television and film describe
the development of each medium over the past twenty years.
Writers now move between the three with a freedom that would
have been unthinkable at the end of the 1970s. To understand the
changes that have taken place it was necessary to look at the performing arts as a whole rather than in isolation. Each chapter
contains an analysis of a single writer's work, with the exception
of the one on television which includes two such examples. The
purpose is twofold. In order to cover the ground as a whole – to
make the cultural journey which I have tried to trace between
Liverpool and Los Angeles – I had to be selective. A more comprehensive account of new writing in theatre, television and film
would have filled at least three volumes which was not my purpose. A proper look at the impact of Irish writing on our theatres,

for instance, would have required a chapter of its own.

There is also scant mention of the dramatists Max Stafford-Clark encouraged at the Royal Court during the 1980s, partly because I wanted to raise the seldom-asked question of what good writing actually is, to be partisan. I do think some writers are better than others. One or two of my choices may surprise or even anger the reader. I am happy if they do: we are losing the capacity to disagree with each other in an interesting way. The writers I have chosen to discuss in detail are David Hare, Dennis Potter, Alan Bleasdale and Mike Leigh. The body of work represented by each of these talents would not have existed without a patron. All four have been supported by a theatre or broadcaster over a number of years in a way that may not be possible for the next generation. The way our attitude to talent is changing – how we are beginning to envy and distrust it – is a further theme.

I hope the book has benefited from my professional life in television. The critical judgements are my own but have been written against the background of having worked as a script editor and producer in the BBC's drama department and as Head of Television Drama at Channel 4 since 1987. I have to thank three of the assistants in the drama department at Channel 4 for organizing my viewing and reading while writing the book. They are Georgia Cheales, Melanie Lindsell and Becky Shaw. But for having enabled me to turn theory into practice and for encouraging, as opposed to stifling, strong opinions among his workforce I'd like to thank Michael Grade.

Peter Ansorge, London 1996

1 Liverpool – London – Los Angeles

Dark ages come, you know, it's a fact, and people don't notice.
Not then. They sit there at home, convinced they're well hidden
away and protected, thinking, 'Jesus Christ, it's getting bad out
there, but this too shall pass.'

– Alan Bleasdale, *GBH*

In recent years it has become fashionable to denigrate the work of
our best-known playwrights. Of course they'd never had a particularly easy ride. The plays of John Osborne, Harold Pinter, Samuel
Beckett and Arnold Wesker counted as many detractors among
their first audiences as they did supporters. But the post-1956 wave
of new British playwrights also won acclaim from a small but
influential section of the press, radio and television. The media – as
they are now known – were not hostile to the idea that the individual voice of a writer might set the cultural agenda for a whole
nation. Plays like *Waiting for Godot* (1955) and *Look Back in
Anger* (1956) became part of a wider debate about the future of
theatre and the direction in which we were or, in the case of
Godot, were not headed. A decade later the discussion was
extended to television drama with the flourishing of *The
Wednesday Play* on the BBC. Drama became acknowledged as
something we were good at.

Over the past ten years newspapers and politicians have sought
to counter this view. British theatre has been asked to question
the relatively small subsidies that have fuelled its post-war revival
in favour of pursuing international success at the box office. The
BBC has been reviled, attacked and is currently, like television as
a whole, undergoing a radical transformation. We have fallen in
love with satellite, cable, video and computers; increasingly out of
love with the notion that drama should challenge as well as entertain. A crucial factor has been the willingness of writers to produce original work across the three disciplines of theatre, film
and television. Few can rely on only one medium either to win a

reputation or to earn a living. The influence of television drama
on writers has been as decisive as the new work being staged at
the Royal Court or National Theatre. Even more pivotal has been
the impact of the feature film. From Robert Bolt (*Doctor
Zhivago*, 1965, and *A Man for All Seasons*, 1966) to Harold
Pinter (*The Servant*, 1963, and *Accident*, 1966), a previous generation chose the screen for adaptation and the stage for original
writing. But no young writer today seeking a career in what the
Americans call the entertainment industry would wish to ignore
the opportunities offered by the success of low-budget feature
films like *My Beautiful Laundrette*, *Four Weddings and a Funeral*
or *Trainspotting*.

The ability to move easily between theatre, film and television
has led to a loss in terms of the relationship between roots and
writing.The single-authored work occupies a less confident place
in our culture than it did twenty years ago. It is a sense of place
that underpins a great many of the best works described in later
chapters: without it drama turns into another forgettable blip or
digit on the super-information highway. But first we begin in the
cities of Liverpool, London and Los Angeles in an attempt to draw
a map of playwriting today.

Liverpool

Arriving in Liverpool in the mid-1990s must feel like London after
the blitz. The buildings still stand, with the exception of the abandoned tower blocks of the 1960s that are being demolished
because they are not safe and no one can bear to live in them. In
the arcades and malls you're struck by how many men are out
shopping or minding the babies, until you realize that this is the
only occupation left to them. They stand outside Kirkby's shopping centre waiting in bewilderment for buses. The transport system has been totally privatized and each afternoon the buses
change owners as they do timetables. The majority of the taxis
have scoured-out interiors and exhausted seating arrangements.
Two or three drivers usually share and pay for one cab, as Terry

Sullivan did for a while in *Brookside*. There are queues of these cabs waiting outside Lime Street for the solitary passengers from London who emerge from first-class railway compartments on weekday mornings. Just before the train weaves into the station you pass over Runcorn Bridge, where Jim Nelson overcame his fear of crossing bridges and literally started to fly in the final moments of Alan Bleasdale's *GBH*.

In Willy Russell's *John, Paul, George, Ringo . . . and Bert* (1974), the hero comments on how hard it is to escape the working-class ghettos of Liverpool. Bert is a drop-out and failure though a life-long fan of the Fabulous Four who did manage to make the break during the 1960s. He is grateful to the Beatles for having presented his generation with a new opportunity. There used to be just two ways, he tells us, for working-class children to escape their background. There was either 'the footy', leading the team out at Anfield and being hailed by the Kop, or the choice that Russell's own heroine took so memorably in *Educating Rita*: education. Now, in pop music, the Beatles had created a third possible route. It is how Bert plans his own escape in the play but unfortunately his skills at the guitar never match those of his idols. He can only dream of leaving while observing at a distance the success of others.

Twenty years on, Bert's options appear to have narrowed. We now look back on the era of the Beatles with a mixture of awe and disbelief. Their success seems unobtainable today; British bands, even in the case of the much-hyped Oasis, no longer achieve the kind of universal fame enjoyed by the Beatles or the Rolling Stones. Meanwhile education is no longer the panacea it once seemed to Bert. The liberal and humane teachers that feature in many of Willy Russell's plays – especially *Educating Rita* and his 1976 television film *Our Day Out* – have been usurped by Jimmy McGovern's bitter 1990s anti-hero in *Hearts and Minds* (1995, Channel 4), whose one-man struggle to improve conditions at a Liverpool comprehensive school ends only in exhaustion and self-disgust. After a decade of hooliganism and the departure of Kenny Dalglish, even the image of Liverpool Football Club seems tarnished – though this is the one item on Bert's list that is as meaningful an escape route today as it was during the 1960s.

He might have added another. For there is one area in which the city has excelled and that Bert clearly failed to identify two decades ago: namely the writing of stage and television plays. The city's economic and social decline has run parallel to a remarkable productivity on the part of its writers. Alan Bleasdale and Willy Russell are two of the country's most successful dramatists. Their work was first presented at the Liverpool Playhouse and Everyman during the 1970s in a unique theatrical moment that was to have enormous consequences for both television and film in the 1980s. Bleasdale went on to write the most influential television drama of the 1980s, *The Boys From the Blackstuff*, and with *GBH* (1991) and *Jake's Progress* (1995) he took over the mantle as our leading television dramatist from the late Dennis Potter. Willy Russell's stage plays such as *Educating Rita* (1978) and *Shirley Valentine* (1986) have won international success. His musical, *Blood Brothers*, first written in the early 1980s, is still running in the West End and on Broadway.

Russell and Bleasdale both live and write in Liverpool. Unique among their generation of writers, they are also recognized by the public. Often mistaken for one another – to the irritation of both – they nevertheless have an entirely individual relationship with the city. However, neither would regard himself as being a Liverpudlian writer – and you wouldn't be invited into either of their homes if you suggested that their work actually contained similar themes. But in one way at least they are different from their London counterparts. David Hare and Howard Brenton have expressed frustration that they seem to have no successors. 'When Stoppard or Pinter looked behind their backs they saw us coming up,' says Hare. 'When Howard or I look back we see no one – no young writers coming up to challenge what we stood for.'

When Bleasdale and Russell look back, they see a host of claimants to their throne. Among their own peers Bill Morrison, author of the formidable *Flying Blind* (still one of our best stage plays about Northern Ireland), and Jim Morrison (*Blood on the*

Dole) stand out. Equally impressive are the newcomers, led by Jimmy McGovern who has catapulted himself into the première league with his TV series, *Cracker* (1993–95) and *Hearts and Minds*, as well as his feature film, *Priest* (1995). McGovern began writing professionally after having abandoned a career in teaching (as did Bleasdale and Russell). During the 1980s he wrote exclusively for *Brookside*, the Channel 4 soap opera which is set on a newly built housing estate on the outskirts of Liverpool. The serial is written by a team of writers who are all Liverpool-based. Apart from McGovern, who quickly gained a reputation for writing the toughest and most controversial episodes of *Brookside*, the programme has produced an array of talent. Currently, Maurice Bessman, Shaun Duggan and Joe Ainsworth are developing their own individual voices on the show as McGovern, Frank Cottrell-Boyce and Frank Clarke (*Letter to Brezhnev*) did before them. *Brookside* at its best has always been regarded as a ground-breaking soap and it certainly predated *Eastenders* in its tackling of controversial issues such as rape, unemployment and teenage sex. Yet the proliferation of playwrights in Liverpool is not confined to the small screen. The Playhouse continues to première the work of new writers from the North West (a recent discovery being Andy Cullen's remarkable *Self-Catering*, 1994, and *Scousers*, 1997). Jonathan Harvey has kept the Scouse flag flying in London by moving from the fringe to the West End with *Beautiful Thing*, the film version of the play following some eighteen months later in 1996.

   Brookside is the creation of Phil Redmond, the Liverpudlian chief executive of Mersey Television who has had his own plays produced at the Playhouse. When Bleasdale or Russell walk the streets of the city they are as likely to be hailed as the authors of *Brookside* ('When they going to dig the body up, Al?') as of *Blackstuff* or *Educating Rita*. The city seems to produce playwrights effortlessly and in a quantity unknown since Jacobean London.

   The writers play down the presence of the city in their work. Yet, undoubtedly, Bleasdale, Russell and McGovern's work, like

Alun Owen and Carla Lane's before them, is infused with a knowledge of a popular audience – a sense of comedy and therefore a confidence to break taboos – often in shorter supply across the rest of the United Kingdom. If you ask them why new writing flourishes in the city the answers vary. All refer to the now defunct port – that one-time gateway to the Atlantic and Ireland. There is a strong Irish presence in the city and it also has the longest established black and Chinese communities in the UK. After the Second World War men working the North Atlantic would bring back news of the latest developments in music. Shops began to sell bootleg US records straight off the boats or from the American airforce base at Warrington. It was often the first place to hear the latest American music: New Orleans jazz, then the crooners like Johnny Ray and Guy Mitchell, finally the first rock-'n'-rollers led by Elvis (about whom Bleasdale has written a stage musical *Are You Lonesome Tonight?*), Gene Vincent and Eddie Cochrane. The latter's death in a car accident after his appearance at the Liverpool Empire has become something of a mythical moment in the town's history and the subject of Bill Morrison's fine stage play *Be Bop A Lula*. The cultural mix does in part explain the real birth of English pop music in the 1960s which is so lovingly described by Bert in Willy Russell's musical. In those days the bars and clubs of the town flowed with the songs of new groups, the patter of stand-up comedy, the poetry of Roger McGough, Adrian Henri and Brian Patten. Liverpool loves language – spoken or sung rather than written down – and for a time the whole country applauded.

During the 1980s everything changed as the city became the number one urban target on Mrs Thatcher's hit list. Recession swept Liverpool before the rest of the country. The Boys From the Blackstuff became the new spokesmen for Merseyside. Bleasdale's dole-struck hero Yosser Hughes's cry of 'Gizza a job' joined 'You'll never walk alone' as a favourite anthem of the Anfield Kop. By the end of the 1980s the population of the city had declined by almost a third and a quarter of the men and women who remained were out of work. Liverpool writers, led by Bleasdale, began to describe a generation born to live by their wits, literally surviving on the edge (or *On the Ledge* in Bleasdale's 1993 National Theatre play) of society – heading towards breakdown even as they're coming up with their funniest lines.

Yet Bleasdale, Russell and McGovern still make Liverpool their home. Unlike a previous generation of successful Northern writers who came south to buy houses in Hampstead, they remain loyal to their roots. In conversation they do not stress deprivation or poverty. They lead good family lives. Phil Redmond is ever anxious to point out that *Brookside* is an aspirational soap, set on a comfortable modern estate where people can improve their lives, a world apart from inner-city decay. In this sense Liverpool stands for a whole tradition of popular writing set outside London. Its greatest impact has often been through television rather than the theatre. Though it may be accused of presenting working-class life in a predictable or sentimental way, the truth is very different. Bleasdale's sense of comedy, for instance, is not a sweetener he supplies to make his harsher themes more palatable; it comes out of the lives he chooses to portray. *Blackstuff* is infused with the pain and indignity of unemployment, but it does not amount to a simple critique of Thatcher's Britain. By the time Bleasdale wrote *Jake's Progress* a decade later, the recession had moved on to middle-class householders, Yosser's madness perhaps now only a mortgage repayment away. In *GBH* the extremes of right- and left-wing politics meet and merge through the madness of council leader Michael Murray until he can no longer be certain of anything. 'The further left you go, the more right-wing you become' became the line that infuriated Bleasdale's left-wing critics, though they failed to notice that in the same year – 1989 – a thousand other Michael Murrays were experiencing a similar nervous breakdown in Eastern Europe after the fall of the Berlin Wall.

Jimmy McGovern often cites the collapse of his own belief in socialism as the catalyst that turned him from a good jobbing writer on *Brookside* into something more. Throughout the 1980s McGovern wrote tellingly about the Grant family in *Brookside*,

Bobby Grant being a militant trade unionist with whom McGovern
clearly sympathized. After leaving *Brookside* it was some while
before McGovern was able to create an equally vivid character on
screen, and when he did so it was in a very different vein. The
character of Fitz in *Cracker* was another study of a man at the
edge: a criminal psychologist, gambler and alcoholic, hating himself for once having believed that men and women can change. His
genius for trapping murderers is by getting them to confess to their
crimes. This he achieves by first looking into himself for the
motive: almost everyone is a potential serial killer, he suspects, so
first to *understand* the crime is the way to expose the criminal. He
has little else to believe in, his faith in both Catholicism and socialism having long since been shattered. The only confession that Fitz
now trusts is that of the criminal. Robbie Coltrane's intelligent and
acerbic performance as Fitz caught the imagination of viewers in
the way that Bleasdale's Yosser Hughes and Michael Murray had
also done. The collapse of certainty in the country at large has been
a key theme of the period. For that purpose Liverpool has been an
ideal location and its best writers the perfect vanguard.

London

> God. Where are you? I wish you would talk to me. There's a
> general feeling. This is what people are saying in the parish.
> They want to know where you are. The joke wears thin. You
> must see that. You never say anything. All right, people expect
> that, it's understood. But people also think. I didn't know when
> he said *nothing*, he really did mean absolutely nothing at all.
> You see, I tell you, it's this perpetual absence – yes? – this not
> being here – it's that – I mean let's be honest – it's just beginning
> to get some of us down.
>
> – David Hare, *Racing Demon*

David Hare's *Racing Demon* (1990) is set in South London, a
favourite location of playwrights over the past decade. Several of

our most successful low-budget feature films have also been shot
there rather than in the more fashionable boroughs of the north.
South London provides the backdrop to Hanif Kureishi's *My
Beautiful Laundrette*, for instance, and to Howard Brenton's stage
plays, *Thirteenth Night* (1981) and *Berlin Bertie* (1992). When a
film-maker like Mike Leigh does turn his camera on North London
– as with the King's Cross of *High Hopes* – it is on an equally
anonymous and desolate landscape. And when David Hare's entrepreneur Tom Sergeant enters the flat of his ex-mistress Kyra Hollis
in *Skylight* (1995), he comments in horror that she has chosen 'to
live in near-Arctic conditions somewhere off the North Circular'.
London as depicted by Brenton, Leigh or Hare – unlike Bleasdale
or Russell's Liverpool – has no particular sense of pride or place
attached to it. It is a no-man's-land, often seen as a wilderness forgotten or abandoned by the rest of the country – as it has been by
God in *Racing Demon*.

London still enjoys the reputation of being the theatrical capital
of the world, but few of its writers are able to infuse either the city
or its stages with any real glamour. The West End theatre, of
course, is rarely able to support the work of new writers at first
hand. In the summer of 1996 practically the only new plays entic-
ing audiences into Shaftesbury Avenue or the Strand were a consequence of the English Stage Company at the Royal Court having to
abandon its headquarters in Sloane Square while extensive rebuild-
ing was taking place. Apart from Harold Pinter's *Ashes to Ashes*
and Jez Butterworth's *Mojo* (both Royal Court productions), there
was only Diane Samuels's *Kindertransport* at the Vaudeville and
Christopher Hampton's translation of Yasmina Reza's *Art* at
Wyndham's.

Yet compare the summer of 1996 in the West End with those of
ten and twenty years earlier. Between June and September 1986
half a dozen new plays were given West End runs. This might not
seem a great contrast with today, but the presence of *The Normal
Heart*, *Stepping Out*, *Circe and Bravo* and David Williamson's
Sons of Cain at least paid lip-service to the idea of a new play culture in the West End. Go back another decade and a very different

picture emerges: between June and September 1976 more than ten new plays were presented. The inclusion in the mainstream of works like *Equus* (admittedly a transfer from the National), Mike Stott's *Funny Peculiar* and Simon Gray's *Otherwise Engaged* suggests a more substantial support for new work. Among the summer premières was one of the last new plays to be presented by H. M. Tennent: *The Family Dance* by Felicity Browne. The majority of critics laughed it out of court – but it is a reminder of a time when West End managers could finance, produce and promote new work. Even more significantly, only six musicals were running in the West End during the summer of 1976. Just two – *A Chorus Line* and *Jesus Christ Superstar* – could claim to be truly large-scale. The others included more intimate works like *Salad Days* and *Side By Side By Sondheim*. Contrast this with the summer of 1996 in a West End where no less than seventeen lavish musicals were competing for an ever diminishing tourist and local audience. It is the enormous number of musicals as opposed to plays that now open each year which has shifted the balance in the West End. The truth is that since the late 1970s new plays have been premièred almost exclusively in small auditoria or pub theatres. The Royal Court, its Theatre Upstairs, the Bush, the Hampstead Theatre Club, the National's Cottesloe and the Royal Shakespeare Company's tiny Pit have been the main platforms for launching the best new work.

The majority of the work has therefore been written for small spaces with tiny casts. The Bush and Theatre Upstairs in particular have pioneered a style of playwriting that is economical in the extreme. Short scenes, time and place fragmented by swift lighting changes, the minimum of scenery: a new play culture has emerged that at times can appear hermetically sealed off from the outside. This is in direct contrast to the fringe theatre of twenty years ago which often came about in active opposition to the work being presented at the National, Royal Court or Royal Shakespeare Company. Actors, directors and writers became involved in the fringe as a first step – or so they imagined – before storming the citadels of the larger subsidized companies or even the West End.

The fringe has now become an end in itself – practically the only producer of new writing.

Inevitably, this has affected the nature of the plays: the central vision has become small-scale. In this respect Max Stafford-Clark's time at the Royal Court during the 1980s is significant. Apart from Caryl Churchill's work, there were few first nights that were able to compete with the finest memories of past regimes. The majority of plays ran for very limited seasons, with a huge reliance on favourable notices in *Time Out* (London's listings magazine) to gain any kind of audience at all. They increasingly appealed to audiences who merely wanted their political prejudices confirmed. In this way the profile of new writing began to change. There was nothing to compare with the impact of Osborne or Wesker's work under George Devine and Tony Richardson, no innovation of style or content that could match William Gaskill's early direction of Edward Bond's *Saved* or Lindsay Anderson's success with the work-plays of David Storey.

Good actors have worked at the Court in the past decade, but where – at least in terms of public recognition – are the equivalents of Frank Finlay, Robert Stephens, Colin Blakely, Alan Bates, Mark MacManus, Victor Henry, Jack Shepherd, Brian Glover, Billie Whitelaw, Nicol Williamson, Judy Parfitt, Helen Mirren or Antony Sher? All gave memorable performances or even made their reputations in new plays premièred at the Royal Court during the 1950s, 1960s and 1970s. During the same decades Laurence Olivier, John Gielgud, Ralph Richardson and Paul Scofield also remade their careers by performing in new work at the Court. Their kind of charismatic performance has been largely absent from new plays in recent years. The performers have become small-scale alongside the plays.

We have had to look elsewhere – to Irish and American plays – for a true reminder of the best traditions of the Court. David Mamet's *Glengarry Glen Ross* and Tony Kushner's *Angels in America* stand out as epic works in the repertory of the National Theatre over the past two decades. Bill Bryden's actors in the Mamet play inhabited the characters and engaged audiences in the finest Royal Court tradition. In John Lahr's words, Kushner's *Angels* honoured the gay community by setting the play against 'the larger historical context of American political life'. On the other hand, Jonathan Harvey in both *Beautiful Thing* and *Babies* is only able to explore his gay characters against the minutiae of an increasingly parochial London landscape. The work of Frank McGuinness, Brian Friel and Sebastian Barry has therefore been a powerful reminder of what has often been missing in English writing of the period. The Irish have managed to conceive work on the same imaginative plane as *Angels* or *Glengarry*, and the performers have often been as powerful as the plays. Barry's *The Steward of Christendom* created a central role for Donal McCann that remained equally powerful for audiences at the Upstairs and downstairs performances at the Royal Court. It echoed the craggy power and urgency of the great Beckett performances.

At the Royal Shakespeare Company, the artistic director Adrian Noble has become increasingly reluctant to entrust the main stage to new plays. Richard Nelson's work, for instance, has been for the most part confined to the smallest stages. Richard Eyre at the National had a far healthier track record in this respect. The Olivier and Lyttelton theatres have seen new work from David Hare, Tony Kushner, Alan Bennett, Tony Harrison and Tom Stoppard among others. Jim Cartwright's *Little Voice* and Patrick Marber's *Dealer's Choice* both began in the Cottesloe but later transferred to the West End. The higher profile enjoyed by the National during this period had a lot to do with Eyre's championing of the new as well as the old.

It can be argued, of course, that new writing is not the priority of a company that is committed to the works of Shakespeare or the classical repertoire. But this is to neglect a critical aspect of, for instance, the RSC's early history. Under Peter Hall and Peter Brook in the 1960s, a turning point in the company's fortunes came with the success of two productions. Brook's *King Lear* (1962) and Hall's *The Wars of the Roses* (1963), an adaptation with John Barton of Shakespeare's *Henry VI* plays and *Richard III* performed over three nights, won acclaim from the public and critics because they were the first post-war performances of Shakespeare to be infused with a contemporary sensibility. Brook's *Lear* acknowledged Samuel Beckett's *Waiting for Godot* and *Endgame* as a major source of inspiration for the design and interpretation of the show which had Paul Scofield in the lead. Hall drew on a whole range of modern texts and sources to work with his actors on making Shakespeare's history plays resonant of the twentieth century's political return to barbarism in the form of Hitler and Stalin. Both directors paid tribute to Jan Kott's recently published *Shakespeare Our Contemporary* (1964), which drew analogies between the politics of Elizabethan England and Eastern Europe and also made references to contemporary playwrights like Brecht, Ionesco and Jean Genet as well as Beckett.

More than thirty years later the argument looks tired and familiar. It is hard now to understand the excitement and controversy that this approach aroused in the early 1960s. But it convinced Peter Hall that contemporary writers were as important to the development of the RSC as Shakespeare. It was a policy that led the company through its most successful years. Two years later a whole generation of students were queuing round the corner of the Aldwych Theatre in the Strand (a far more appealing London home for the RSC than the Barbican ever became) for David Warner's *Hamlet* and Peter Brook's *Marat/Sade* starring the young Glenda Jackson. Harold Pinter was soon to become Peter Hall's other house dramatist. During his subsequent regime at the National, Hall's most memorable hits were often original plays: *Pravda*, *Weapons of Happiness*, *Amadeus* and *Plenty*.

This is a message that the young directors of the 1980s and 1990s have largely forgotten: they often overlook the fact that there are rules for directing both classical and modern works. Not every decision can be a result of mere directorial whimsy. In 1962 Peter Brook was severely castigated for cutting a scene in *King Lear* that critics regarded as crucial to Shakespeare's intention. Brook took the interval after Gloucester's blinding rather than the traditional first curtain after the storm scene. He cut the rebellion of Cornwall's servant against the on-stage blinding, leaving a sightless Gloucester helplessly trying to find his way like Pozzo at the end of *Godot* just as the interval lights came up. The loss of the servant's protest meant that the universe of the play appeared more pitiless and godless than most critics thought appropriate; some inkling of humanity had been lost, they claimed. One or two even wanted to take the RSC's subsidy away because of this relatively minor departure from the text. Such a controversy is unthinkable today. Sixteen years after the storm caused by Brook's interpretation, I saw Adrian Noble's own Stratford-upon-Avon production of the play with Michael Gambon as the King. In the hovel scene Gambon's crazed Lear grabbed a cushion and proceeded to suffocate Antony Sher's Fool to death. He then tipped the corpse into a dustbin. The moment was universally praised by reviewers. Quite possibly it did explain the Fool's mysterious absence from the rest of the play, but it did little to justify the making of a murderer out of Shakespeare's leading character. As a result the audience had very little sympathy for Gambon's King during the later and most moving scenes (an error Noble was to correct in his 1993 revival of *Lear* with Robert Stephens). Brook's production was held together by a vision of the play that was rooted in the work and understanding of a great contemporary writer. Noble's invention was a purely directorial whim; it had no basis in what we seriously think about the play today.

The mid-1980s saw the emergence of a very talented crop of new directors, but one that follows the Noble rather than the Hall line on new writing and classical revivals. Deborah Warner, Declan Donnellan, Stephen Pimlott, Matthew Warchus, Phyllida Lloyd, Stephen Daldry and Sam Mendes have all won their reputations through classical revivals or with plays and musicals from the very recent past. They are Thatcher's children, not on a political but an aesthetic plane. None is closely identified with a living writer in the tradition of Hall and Pinter, Peter Wood and Tom Stoppard, Michael Blakemore and Peter Nichols or William Gaskill and Edward Bond. It is true that Warchus is the director of *Art* while Phyllida Lloyd has directed both Terry Johnson's *Hysteria* and John Guare's *Six Degrees of Separation* at the Royal Court, but she won her spurs at the National, like Warchus, with her growing reputation in opera and the classics. Declan Donnellan directed *Angels in America* at the National but he is best known as the creator of Cheek By Jowl who specialize in revivals. This has been a loss to British theatre over the past decade. If it is not fuelled by the imagination and experience of a living writer, one's memory of a production fades more easily. In the way that spectacle dominates the West End theatre through *Cats*, *The Phantom of the Opera* and *Starlight Express*, so it does our subsidized stages. Daldry's *An Inspector Calls* and Warchus's *Volpone* were undoubtedly stunning theatrical events, evoking a Thatcherite obsession with private capital and greed in both J. B. Priestley's London and Ben Jonson's Venice. But an audience went away from those shows, if not – in Michael Billington's memorable phrase about Lloyd Webber musicals – humming the sets, then certainly thinking as much about them as the plays. Deborah Warner was taken to task by the *Guardian* for confessing that she won't direct plays by living writers because they are always 'neurotic'. In reply she stated: 'I would love to direct a new play when there are new plays of the size that is offered to me in classics . . . one you could give a year of your life to' (*Guardian*, 21 September 1991).

In Stephen Fay's biography of Peter Hall, *Power Play*, it is stated that in 1953 West End managers commissioned and financed twenty-six new plays, a number that is inconceivable today when stars cannot be tempted to commit to long runs and directors like Deborah Warner might demand a year's rehearsal period. In 1953, of course, most of those plays would have had common settings, with characters from exclusively middle-class and upper-middle-class backgrounds. As Kenneth Tynan wrote of the typical play of the day: 'The setting is in a country house in what used to be called Loamshire, but now, as a heroic tribute to realism, is sometimes called Berkshire.' We now look back on those days with a smile of superiority. Yet writers then held a far more powerful position in West End theatre than they do now. There was a greater variety of new work being presented, properly resourced and managed. It is for these reasons that younger directors may prefer to revive Rattigan, Coward or Priestley rather than having to depend on a pub environment in which to present new plays by their peers. Certainly they do not seem to be giving writers the kind of resources that a classic play now commands.

Theatre is not the only outlet for playwrights in London. To the west of the capital lies the BBC's White City base, dominated by a rotund building from the 1960s which is the model for the scientific laboratory in Dennis Potter's final television serial, *Cold Lazarus* (1996). It is 400 years into the future, and a group of scientists are being starved of vital resources and cash to finance their experiments – undoubtedly Potter's metaphor for what is happening to writers and producers in today's BBC.

With its two television channels and five radio stations, the BBC has been the greatest patron of new writers that this country and possibly the world has ever known. When I first joined the Corporation in 1976 as a script editor in the television drama department at Birmingham's Pebble Mill, there were over fifty producers in London and the regions commissioning drama. Heads of departments were entrusted with generous development budgets and separate responsibilities. The demarcation zones between single plays, series and serials were clearly marked and established. The output included some of the most challenging and yet accessible work ever seen by a television audience, as well as a fair amount of kitsch on Sunday evenings. Twenty years ago there were dozens of outlets for single plays, with a variety of producers commissioning them. At best *Play for Today* on BBC1 could win audiences of well over 10 million, easily matching the viewing figures for the most popular series and serials.

Possibly the BBC's output never rivalled the impact or strength of the best Royal Court plays. But with *Wednesday Plays* like Ken Loach's *Cathy Come Home* and Potter's *Vote, Vote, Vote for Nigel Barton* it came a close second during the 1960s. In the 1980s the great original television serials, such as *The Boys From the Blackstuff*, *The Singing Detective* and *Edge of Darkness*, put BBC drama ahead of any equivalent writing event in the theatre. However, in the 1990s the BBC began to experience a period of unparalleled change and uncertainty. Faced with having to make a case to the government for the continuation of the licence fee, it had to argue that it was a billion-pound business rather than a purely public-service broadcaster. Huge upheavals took place within the organization, often bewildering the writers and producers working there. At the same time audiences on BBC1 began to slump, faced with heavy competition – particularly in drama – from the newly restructured ITV companies. As a consequence of the 1992 Broadcasting Bill, the commissioning of all drama on the ITV network became the responsibility of a Network Centre based at the old *Sunday Times* building in London's Gray's Inn Road. The streamlining of decision-making had an immediate effect. Thrillers began to dominate primetime viewing, gaining huge popularity and critical acclaim in the case of *Prime Suspect*, *Cracker* and *Inspector Morse*. The old hierarchies at the BBC began to crumble as the channel controllers took over the reins of commissioning from heads of drama in order to compete in a ratings war with ITV.

The BBC and ITV still commission hundreds of hours of original drama every year, but there is a far narrower range of work being produced. The freedoms offered by the single plays of the 1960s and 1970s have long since disappeared. New writers must learn their craft by writing successfully for the soaps or police thrillers in the first instance. This is not in itself a creative hardship. After all, both John McGrath and Troy Kennedy Martin wrote their first television scripts on *Z Cars*, while Jimmy McGovern served an eight-year apprenticeship on *Brookside* before developing his own work. The difference is that it is now almost impossible to find in the primetime schedules of either BBC1 or ITV a drama that isn't a thriller, hospital show or, more recently, a Jane Austen adaptation. Fifteen years ago there would have been a greater variety of drama: a mix of thrillers, adaptations, single plays, classic and modern serials which served the viewer in generous and unexpected ways. No wonder a generation of writers and directors are spurning television and theatre to find other excitement in a third city – Los Angeles.

Los Angeles

Well – isn't that rather the point? Isn't that what my script's
about? Karaoke! As a metaphor, I mean. The music's written
and performed by someone else, and there's this piddling little
space left for you to sing yourself, but only to *their* lyrics, *their*
timing.

– Dennis Potter, *Karaoke*

The Sunset Maquis Hotel in West Hollywood is famous for playing host to rock bands. Residents are frequently woken at two in
the morning to the splash of a lead guitarist being thrown into the
swimming pool. At midday, however, when iced tea and Caesar
salads are being served on the patio, with the sun adding its white
brush strokes, the blue of the pool is pure Hockney – one of the
attractions, perhaps, for British visitors. For it is to Los Angeles
during the 1980s that British directors and writers came in
increasing numbers to work on screenplays, make deals and gener-
ally to dream the impossible dream. It is the idea of Hollywood
rather than the reality which attracts British talent. Hockney saw
in the light of the Hollywood hills an escape from the drabness of
his Bradford upbringing. So too do British directors and writers
imagine an escape from the confines of our theatre and television.
It is the dream of Los Angeles rather than the reality with which
this book is concerned.

Colin Welland once announced at a much-discussed Oscar ceremony that the British were coming to Hollywood. Other than his
own presence, I doubt whether he believed it. Yet the success of a
handful of low-budget feature films, financed by a British television company, was to make a stop at the Sunset Maquis or
Beverley Wilshire a practical and sometimes profitable new career
move for the Brits. During the 1970s it was commonplace to speak
of the British film industry being alive and well and working in
television. Directors like Stephen Frears, Mike Newell, Mick
Jackson and later Jon Amiel practised their craft through one-off

films or serials for the BBC or ITV. It was the advent of Channel 4, with its policy of showing made-for-television films in the cinema, that proved a turning point. In the mid-1980s films like *My Beautiful Laundrette*, *Letter to Brezhnev* and *Wish You Were Here*, financed by Channel 4, were shown in cinemas and won worldwide acclaim. A decade later Channel 4 backed *Four Weddings and a Funeral* which became the most successful British film ever made. After directing *The Singing Detective* for the BBC, Jon Amiel was able to exchange a White City career for one in Hollywood. He was soon followed by Mick Jackson, who was turning over on *LA Story* a year after his Channel 4 mini-series, *A Very British Coup*, won huge acclaim in the States. Many of our strongest directorial talents have been lost to Hollywood in the past ten years, though some – most notably Stephen Frears – still attempt to commute between the two cultures.

British directors now consider a successful first play, feature or even ten-minute short as a calling card to Hollywood. This has led to a downgrading of the writer in favour of the director. What point is there in backing a new talent at the Theatre Upstairs when you can be directing a car chase on the Santa Monica freeway? Hollywood pays writers exceptionally well but the majority are discarded during the production process. Rewriting other people's scripts is as well paid an activity in LA as writing your own; indeed it is probably the more secure job in the long run. Does our recent embrace of the cinema disguise an irritation with the single-voiced play or television serial? In our new-found love affair with the movies, how far are we in flight from meaning and debate in pursuit of pure entertainment? This was after all the great distinction that Sir Huw Wheldon once made between British and American television. American television, he claimed, was remarkable in many ways. Highly professional, skilled, popular, a global commodity whose writers had no higher ambition than to entertain. The British in turn could make highly professional and popular television; but we could never turn into a global commodity because we wanted our writers to challenge viewers as well as entertain them.

When Wheldon made those comments he was pretty confident about the role of the BBC and the importance of new writing. People are less confident now. Increasingly, we look to ratings or box-office receipts as the sole criteria for success. A belief in individual talent is being put on the backburner. The debunking of artists, a championing of team-writing techniques, a humourless search for the narrative key that will unlock the secrets of Hollywood movies have become the subject matter of arts programmes and critical writing. This has not always been the case. A previous generation of critics looked back at the century with pride. In the early decades there were the examples of Granville Barker and Shaw. Given the state of West End theatre today, we have little reason to be smug about the success of Coward and Rattigan between the World Wars. Following them came a generation of playwrights that are only surpassed in fame and achievement by the Elizabethans. In the theatre there was Osborne, Pinter, Bond, Beckett, Ayckbourn, Stoppard, Shaffer and Hare. On TV we had David Mercer, Potter, Ken Loach, Alan Bennett, Mike Leigh and Alan Bleasdale. In no other country did the best writers so actively *want* to work for television. Post-war Britain has a poor record in industry and politics. No one has ever claimed that our novelists have the same vitality as their post-war American counterparts. But our playwrights are the envy of the world.

Partly as a result of this, our universities and colleges are overflowing with students engaged in the study of film, television and theatre. Computer software, public relations and screenwriting are likely to be among the key professions of the future as we move towards an increasingly service-based economy. Yet this development is occurring at a time when we are abandoning many of our more vital commitments towards public broadcasting and subsidy of the arts.

One of the themes of Dennis Potter's last serial for television was that of entertainment and the devil's pact. As the entertainment industry expands, so does the power vested in it. How will we relate to a world that is no longer ruled by politicians or even leaders of industry but by entertainment moguls? In *Cold Lazarus*

Potter raises the spectre of a frozen head from the late twentieth century being revived almost 400 years into the future. Science has advanced to the extent that it can project the memories of the frozen head on to a living screen in a scientific laboratory. In common with most science fiction, the future is a world that has outlawed memory and a sense of history. Yet paradoxically Daniel Feeld's memories become that world's most marketable commodity. The scientists watch the past unfolding in a dramatic shape on-screen – like spectators at a play – and they cannot do without it. Neither can their masters or mistresses who compete for the global television rights.

The message is a simple but moving one. We need fiction. The writer who can forge an entertaining link between the past and present will always be in work.

2 Theatre – Public and Private Voices

> To tell the truth even . . . that would be wonderful. If words
> were only their meaning. Well then . . . But words are their
> effect also.
>
> – David Hare, *The Absence of War*

The 1980s witnessed a fight for survival in the theatre that damaged its confidence and power. During that decade the Royal Court
lost ground and struggled to provide the kind of landmark production that had distinguished previous regimes. In the 1960s and
early 1970s it was unquestionably the home of the best new writing
talent. The theatre also proclaimed a concrete artistic policy in its
search for new writing that was begun by the George Devine-Tony
Richardson era and continued by both Lindsay Anderson and
William Gaskill. It was quite an austere philosophy that often
emphasized plain white lighting on stage, and minimalist sets
drawn from raw materials like steel and leather of which the
Court's first great stage designer Jocelyn Herbert was the pioneer.
The influence of both Bertolt Brecht and Samuel Beckett was strong
on the Court's visual style. Plays reflecting working-class life and
favouring actors from non-middle-class backgrounds were also in
fashion. This was a result of the upheaval and controversy caused
by the first generation of Court writers in the 1950s with work like
Osborne's *Look Back in Anger*, Wesker's *Chips With Everything*
and John Arden's *Live Like Pigs*. Anderson and Gaskill carried on
this tradition with consistent backing of the plays of David Storey
and Edward Bond. Younger middle-class playwrights in fact had a
tough time getting their early work on at the Court.

At the Royal Shakespeare Company Harold Pinter was the
leading contemporary writer in favour, alongside the theatre's
championing (with little success at the box office) of the European
absurdist playwrights.The National Theatre had Peter Nichols
and the young Tom Stoppard as its stars in the new-writing firma-

ment. Our three strongest subsidized theatres thus supported different writers and visual styles through their productions, clinging fiercely to their separate artistic identities. When Peter Hall's name was mentioned as the successor to Olivier at the National, Kenneth Tynan protested to the Board: 'We are the Cavaliers, Stratford the Roundheads – with the emphasis on analytic intelligence and textual clarity. Under Peter Hall the country would have two Roundhead theatres.' At the same time a flourishing fringe theatre was producing new writing responsive to the student movement and political questioning of the late 1960s.

During the 1980s all of these theatres, including the fringe, lost their identities, certainly as far as new writing was concerned. With certain exceptions, such as David Hare at the National and Caryl Churchill at the Court, writers were no longer identified with the policies of an individual theatre or director. In fact there were no artistic policies because – as Eliza Doolittle's father says of morals – theatres could no longer afford them. People went where the work was, not to a building that represented an idea of what theatre ought to be. New writing became fragmented and was most often mounted in small spaces with tiny casts. Few could command the design support enjoyed by Hare at the National. Yet ambitious design and epic staging were a crucial factor behind the success of post-war British playwrights, from Osborne's *Luther* to Shaffer's *The Royal Hunt of the Sun* and *Amadeus*. Peter Hall's large-scale productions of Pinter's work at the RSC and National would have been unthinkable without the breadth of designer John Bury's visual imagination. Few who saw the original production of Pinter's *The Homecoming* in the 1960s can forget the choice of furniture, let alone the writing and acting. As we have seen, a younger generation of directors during the 1980s tended to abandon new writing in favour of spectacular productions of the classics. At least that way they got to work on main stages with first-rate designers and could hope to make some kind of real impact on the public and critics.

It should not be forgotten that writers and directors of the 1980s were competing for attention in a cultural environment very

different from the 1960s and 1970s. The rise of the British musical
has been the real event of that decade. From *Cats* to *Evita* and
Sunset Boulevard, Andrew Lloyd Webber and his collaborators
have created a sense of spectacle and occasion which the public
now associates automatically with a good night out. The majority
of playwrights cannot compete and probably would not wish to. I
have taken children to performances of *Cats* and been hugely entertained. I remember looking at the young audiences who flocked to
Evita in the late 1970s, thinking that Hal Prince's kitsch but memorable production had done a great service to the theatre by bringing in audiences who normally only attended rock concerts or
pantomimes. I had failed to see that Lloyd Webber's singular
achievement was to have combined these two previously distinct
genres. Audiences the world over now look upon theatre primarily
as a place to see musicals. Interestingly, the popularity of Broadway
musicals has declined and it is our subsidized theatres that keep
Stephen Sondheim's name in lights rather than the West End. The
National Theatre has become the prime spot for reviving the great
Broadway hits of the past like *Guys and Dolls* or *Carousel*. When
the latter did transfer to the West End for a limited run, it could not
compete with the popularity of *The Phantom of the Opera*.

What is the secret of Lloyd Webber's success? His musicals are
dominated by design concepts: the skating-rink in *Starlight
Express*, the falling chandelier in *Phantom*, the gothic staircase in
Sunset Boulevard. The music is derivative of late nineteenth-cen-
tury opera and mid-1960s pop – easily recognizable and digestible
for audiences that now include as many coach parties from Tokyo
as Wolverhampton. Few critics have actually examined the content
of these musicals. In fact, although they are set in many different
places – *Evita* in Argentina, *Jesus Christ Superstar* in Jerusalem,
Sunset Boulevard in 1940s Los Angeles – they do have one thing in
common: Lloyd Webber has rarely set a successful show in Great
Britain. His musicals take place in a no-man's-land of the imagination. The Argentina of *Evita* and the Paris of *Phantom* are not
based on real places in the way of Sondheim's New York in
Company or even Rodgers and Hammerstein's New England in

Carousel. Unlike the Broadway tradition, they are truly stateless musicals. When he looks at London, Lloyd Webber can only do so through the green eyes of T. S. Eliot's pantomime cats. The musicals have only one theme: the cult of being a celebrity and the price of fame. You might argue that this has been the traditional preoccupation of the musical over the past forty years rather than the more complex themes, for instance, by which Stephen Sondheim seeks to invigorate the form today. But setting such a subject against a Broadway background for a Broadway audience during the 1930s and 1940s was an entirely understandable process. It reflected a real aspiration and optimism on the part of the nation concerned. Lloyd Webber merely seeks to identify the rock star, diva or dictator in each of his characters, unencumbered by any real sense of time or place. In spite of the undoubted theatrical impact, he dehumanizes the form as a consequence.

It is in this sense that one questions the new generation's approach to the classics. Watching Stephen Daldry's production of *An Inspector Calls*, for instance, one is aware of a design concept almost as spectacular as that employed in *The Phantom of the Opera*. Without it you doubt whether Daldry would have been interested in reviving the play. The house that visibly crumbled onstage in Daldry's production equals the shock of the chandelier that the Phantom sends hurtling down on the audience just before the interval of Lloyd Webber's musical. Such resources have simply not been given to new plays during this period. It is perhaps understandable that the profile of new writing has suffered as a result. But it is also possible that working on new plays requires a different approach.

There has been a movement back to new writing in the 1990s. Our theatres still manage to discover an array of new talent each year. Under Stephen Daldry, the Royal Court has returned to the idea that the first night of a new play can be as glamorous an event as a movie première. Jude Kelly's work at the West Yorkshire Playhouse in recent years suggests that the regions may also be undergoing something of a revival. The Bush Theatre has harvested an impressive crop of writers under its artistic directors

Dominic Dromgoole (now working with Peter Hall at the Old Vic) and Mike Bradwell. Yet very few of the plays have entered the general repertoire. When one asks what have been the really exciting new plays, the *vital* turning points in theatre since the beginning of the 1980s – works that have really stirred the audience's imagination and changed their way of looking at the world – the answers are not immediately forthcoming. In February 1996 I attended a performance of a new play at Liverpool's Everyman Theatre. The play, an accessible two-hander, had been well received locally and my companions assumed that the auditorium would be packed. In fact there were eight people in attendance. During the interval our small party sipped luke-warm white wine in the refurbished bar area and reflected on the old days at the Everyman. This was a theatre that under Alan Dossor in the 1970s had one of the most talented acting ensembles in the country. Julie Walters, Jonathan Pryce, Alison Steadman, Bernard Hill, Trevor Eve, Antony Sher and many others began their working lives there in new plays by Willy Russell, Bill Morrison and Alan Bleasdale. The theatre was packed most nights with audiences dominated by students and the working class (the Playhouse up the road played to a posher crowd). In 1996 that audience had long disappeared. Part of the reason had to do with economics. At eight pounds a head, even ticket prices at the Everyman were on the steep side. Students and sixth-formers simply can't afford to make regular visits to the theatre in the way of previous generations. When I was a schoolboy in London my pocket money ran to three upper circle seats a week at the theatre. Now one has to save up for it as a special event. As a result, even in Liverpool people are more likely to choose Lloyd Webber than the new Bill Morrison. So, as we spoke in the interval bar that night, another question raised itself. Perhaps – as Hamlet told Horatio – the fault lay with ourselves rather than the stars. Could it be that the writers had let us down; that the plays, unlike the musicals, just don't entertain any more? It is with this in mind that we will be looking at the work of a writer whose ambitions for theatre have been allowed to exceed by far those of his contemporaries.

David Hare and the National Theatre

David Hare is not alone in having benefited from the support of a single theatre over the past fifteen years. From his home base in Scarborough, Alan Ayckbourn has continued to present West End audiences with a regular diet of intelligent, challenging and sometimes repetitive farces. Tom Stoppard is able to move between the West End and the subsidized sector with ease, as both *Indian Ink* and *Arcadia* have proved. Peter Shaffer and Harold Pinter launch their new plays pretty much on their own terms. Yet we no longer associate the work of these writers with the kind of alliance that William Gaskill struck with Edward Bond or Lindsay Anderson with David Storey at the Royal Court. The famous director–writer partnerships of Peter Hall/Harold Pinter, Michael Blakemore/Peter Nichols, John Dexter/Arnold Wesker and Tony Richardson/John Osborne are now a distant theatrical memory.

So why have I chosen David Hare as my key illustration of theatrical excellence for the purposes of this book? It is often said that his plays are strong on ideas but weak on emotion. Tom Stoppard, Harold Pinter and Alan Bennett are certainly more popular and famous names. To the Ancient Greeks fame did not mean being a celebrity; it meant being acknowledged for your public acts. Being a playwright implied just that: you were judged by the public. If a play was judged a success, it would become part of a debate in which the audience also participated. Audiences at the National who have gone to see Hare's work over the years regard theatre partly in those terms. They may love or hate the plays – that is not my point – but the plays touch issues of the day and public concerns which are inseparable from the art of being a playwright. Hare is almost our last writer within that tradition. Through the backing given to him first by Peter Hall and then Richard Eyre, he has been uniquely able to command the resources of all three stages at the National. If nothing else, the results underline the importance of a long-term commitment on the part of a theatre to a writer. Hare has undoubtedly flourished where others – denied a

patron – have fallen. If the work of new writers is entirely confined
to *ad hoc* spaces at the Bush or Theatre Upstairs, its profile
inevitably declines and no debate follows.

Part of the reason that Hare's work is sometimes judged as cold
is that he writes successfully about middle-class characters and
middle-class institutions. In his very first play, *Slag*, three young
women withdraw from society to work at an exclusive girls'
school called Brackenhurst. Gradually their dreams of finding freedom from men start to crumble. The bitchiness of boarding-school
life, the dirty tricks once learned and now taught on the hockey
pitch, start to take their toll. Twenty-five years later, in *Skylight*,
Hare makes a heroine out of another teacher, Kyra Hollis; but one
who this time has chosen to drop out by teaching at a desperate
inner-city comprehensive in defiance of her fat-cat lover who is
determined to win back her love.

In between, Hare has written about the diplomatic service,
journalism, the law, the Church and parliament – institutions that
are all in decay yet having in the 1980s to face the new brutalism
of Mrs Thatcher's policies. To some degree Terence Rattigan wrote
about these same civil servants and secondary school teachers during the 1940s – with their private griefs, loneliness and glimpses of
heroism – but never with the sustained irony or sense of comedy
that Hare brings to the job. No playwright could survive in the
business if they were really only strong on political ideas and weak
on human emotions. Emotional engagement with an audience is
the real key to any dramatic success. At the climax of *The Secret
Rapture* (1988) there is an astonishing transformation of the set
that transcends anything in Rattigan's drawing-room tragedies.
Marion, a junior minister in Margaret Thatcher's government,
returns to the family house where her father has recently died and
her sister has been murdered. She has no living family apart from
her husband Tom. Only now does she seek to restore the sitting
room to its former state. In a black dress, removing covers from
the furniture and fetching chairs, she recalls her unhappy childhood in front of her husband. Having completed her task, she ges-
tures around the room. The stage directions read that the room 'is

perfectly restored into an English sitting room – furniture, carpets, curtains, ornaments'. 'Yes,' agrees Tom. 'Well done. It's lovely . . . A perfect imitation of life.' The words sent a shock wave around the theatre. Here was a perfect set for a middle-class English audience – the perfect home – but clearly now revealed as an artifice to hide behind. For it is Marion who has drained away life from the house. It is her political anger that is indirectly responsible for the death of her sister.

Hare's plays need that artifice, the shock of fine sets that are suddenly whisked away (as the drawing room was at the end of Howard Davies's production), to make their effect. There is an artifice of drawing-room comedy about *The Secret Rapture*. The first scene takes place in a bedroom where Marion's father has died. Her sister Isobel is sitting by the bed. Marion has come to steal a ring she gave her father; she does not want his new young wife to inherit it. When Isobel catches her out, she refuses to apologize. It is in fact the character of Marion, the bad Tory sister, who drives the play and offers a useful insight into Hare's technique as a political playwright. She is clever, witty, purposeful and, in the opening scene, the most human character. Penelope Wilton's performance in the original production brought a wonderful dynamic of contained anger to the part. For no one actually criticizes Marion for her appalling behaviour: she is hearing censorial voices from somewhere else. Her sister Isobel remains calm, self-contained and usually silent. Her husband Tom comments: 'Her Party's in power. For ever. She's in office. She's an absolute cert for the Cabinet. I just don't see why she's angry all the time.'

It is now that we begin to look at Marion in her public as well as her private role. According to Hare, Mrs Thatcher's appeal lay in her insistence that voters no longer needed a conscience about social policy; they should only judge governments by the economic results. This is the position that Marion takes up in the play. She bullies Isobel into giving their dead father's new wife, the alcoholic Katherine, a job. She is appalled at the suggestion that she might have to find her one herself: 'Don't be ridiculous. I'm in the Conservative Party. We can't just take on anyone at all.' These lines were snapped out brilliantly by Miss Wilton; at every performance they brought the house down. People often refer to this kind of thing in Hare's work as being cheap: an easy joke or smart remark at the expense of a 'good' character which in this case might even create sympathy for a Conservative minister. But lines like these – in a comparatively serious piece about conscience and action – are neither smart nor easy; they are an essential tool of the dramatist. We are presented with a more complex view of the Thatcherite years than we are used to – especially from a left-wing playwright. For Marion's lines are also true to her character. From her point of view the Conservative Party does present a coherent intellectual viewpoint. She and her colleagues do work extremely hard. Later on she is able to explain this to a fellow Tory after a particularly successful encounter with 'the Greens': 'You know, they were expecting an idiot. That's the first mistake. Because you're a Conservative. And a member of the Government. They expect you to be stupid . . . You blast them right out of the water. Hey, at this moment I could take them all on. The gloves are off. That's what's great. That's what's exciting. It's a new age. Fight to the death.'

Racing Demon followed two years later in 1990 and is the first in a trilogy of plays about British institutions. Hare had already included a number of such work places in his plays – from the Stock Exchange in *Knuckle* (1974) to the Foreign Office in *Plenty* (1978) – but never on such a broad or predetermined canvas. The writing of each play was preceded by an intensive period of research and interviews with members of the particular profession under investigation. The results – with the possible exception of the second work in the trilogy, *Murmuring Judges* – were far more successful than Kenneth Tynan's attempts to present a series of 'faction' plays during his tenure at the National Theatre. In particular, *Racing Demon* is a wonderfully imaginative and suspenseful account of the Church of England which takes an audience into dramatic territory that is now uniquely David Hare's.

The leading character is the middle-aged Reverend Lionel Espy. We first see him kneeling on the ground and addressing God in an apologetic manner. The beautifully written and comic opening

speech might indicate that the play we are about to watch is a simple satire on the Church and all its hypocrisies. But nothing could
be further from the truth. Although concentrating on the conspic-
uous absence of God in his South London parish, Espy's speech is
completely sincere: 'I mean, let's be honest – it's just beginning to
get some of us down. You know? Is that unreasonable? There are
an awful lot of people in a very bad way. And they need something
beside silence, God. Do you understand?'

It is hard to disassociate this moment from Oliver Ford Davies's
delivery of the lines in Richard Eyre's original production. Though
the speech is a true account of his personal doubts about God, he
can only articulate them in a deeply embarrassed way. Part of the
crisis in the play stems from Lionel Espy's view that decent English
men and women shouldn't believe anything very strongly in the
first place. Somehow the liberal self-contradictory nature of
English life makes real belief or passion embarrassing – to the
Church and clergy alike. Ford Davies expressed this dilemma phys-
ically by occupying the stage in a permanent condition of hang-dog
embarrassment. He was delighted to accept anyone else's view of
events, beaming at the sight of a mind being made up. When called
on to give his own opinion, he'd seize up in a frown of agonized
depression. A black woman in the parish comes to him for help
with her violent husband, and he tries and fails to give her some
good advice. He proposes that they pray together to God though
she is almost as embarrassed by the action as he is. 'Will that help?'
the woman asks afterwards. 'I don't know,' says Lionel. 'It can't do
any harm.'

This is part of the reason why he is summoned to visit the
Bishop of Southwark. The scene begins before lunch in the palace
garden where, in typical Hare fashion, some rules of establishment
life must first be honoured so that the Bishop can then begin to
question Lionel on his parish. The early talk is of the meal ahead
and the excellence of the Bishop's wife's fishcakes. Does Lionel's
own wife cook? Yes, yes frequently, Lionel replies, nervously trying
to remember. But no serious conversation can take place at lunch,
so the Bishop begins to reveal his hand. An element of the parish

has been to see him. A complaint has been made about Lionel.
Anything specific? asks Lionel. The Bishop replies: 'Extremely specific. They're not sure you still believe in the rules of the club.'

There is no evidence in the play that the Bishop believes any
more strongly in God than Lionel. But what he does believe in are
the rules of 'the club'. They are to be upheld even though the ideas
underwriting them have long since decayed. In this the Bishop of
Southwark belongs to a line of brilliantly conceived establishment
figures in Hare's work. Their view of office is perhaps most
tellingly summarized in *Plenty* by the figure of Sir Andrew
Charleson, Head of Personnel at the Foreign Office. The scene is
set in Whitehall in 1962 and he is addressing the heroine, Susan
Brock:

> That is the nature of the service, Mrs Brock. It is called diplo-
> macy. And in its practice the English lead the world. The irony
> is this: we had an empire to administer, there were six hundred
> of us in this place. Now it's to be dismantled and there are six
> thousand. As our power declines, the fight among us for access
> to that power becomes a little more urgent, a little uglier per-
> haps. As our influence wanes, as our empire collapses, there is
> little to believe in. Behaviour is all.

In *Racing Demon* Lionel has become sceptical about the administration of Communion to his parishioners. He stresses that, like
the Church as a whole, the ceremony 'has no connection with people's lives'. This is of little concern to the Bishop. Like the men
who run the Foreign Office in *Plenty*, he has other priorities: 'Only
one thing unites us. The administration of the sacrament. Finally
that's what you're there for . . . As a priest you have only one duty.
That's to put on a show.'

We are next introduced to the priests on Lionel's team. They
include the younger Reverend Donald 'Streaky' Bacon and the
Reverend Harry Henderson. Both show weariness from working
in their impoverished inner-city parish but, like Lionel, they are
immensely likeable. Donald comes on 'in a duffel coat with bright
orange reflector pads and bicycle clips' complaining about the

behaviour of motorists, while Harry enters with a big McDonald's bag full of 'teas and coffees and apple pies'. He announces that he's having to call in 'the diocesan exorcist' that evening on behalf of a West Indian parishioner. Streaky says that he's rather jealous, never having witnessed an exorcist at work. Harry replies with a twinkle in his eye: 'I know. It's a West Indian lady. With a lot of nocturnal movement. She asked me to stay the night. But I refused . . . I'm going to be shattered if something actually appears.'

When writing about the success or otherwise of a play, this kind of scene is rarely discussed. After all, don't the jokes seem rather obvious and crowd-pleasing? Aren't Donald and Harry – caught with their trousers down and bicycle clips in tow – themselves partly comic vicars from the tradition of West End farce? Isn't this the lowest common denominator side of a supposedly highbrow playwright like David Hare? The truth is that such scenes are a key to the success of any play in the theatre. Getting the audience to laugh at your subject matter means that they are halfway to taking it seriously. Getting them emotionally involved with your characters is the hardest, not the simplest, of tasks. In the original production the entrances of David Bamber's Donald and Michael Bryant's Harry were a triumph for both these reasons. The play had taken us into a world of inner-city collapse and spiritual crisis, but suddenly we were able to spot two familiar and decent landmarks. Donald and Harry are wonderfully loyal to Lionel. Their dishevelled comic presence and support made us love and enjoy Lionel more.

Tony is the fourth member of the parish team, and a very different animal. Like Marion in *The Secret Rapture*, he represents a new kind of character in David Hare's work. Whereas the Bishop wishes to preserve the status quo, Tony wishes to change it through a cruel new wind of belief:

I want a full church. Is that so disgraceful? I want to see the whole community all worshipping under one roof. That's what I want. And that's what I believe the Lord wants as well. I'm the junior member, this is my first parish, I've no right to bring this up, I can tell you, we can go about our business, we can look at our schedules, but really if in three years we don't fill the churches on Sunday, I'm sorry, then I think we'll have failed.

It emerges that Lionel is coming to the end of a five-year free-lance contract with the Church and can be dismissed. This is the Bishop's secret agenda and he intends to use Tony's criticism of the parish to justify his action. In this way the microcosm of the Church starts to mirror the way many other middle-class institutions were headed throughout the 1980s. Hospitals, universities, schools, banks, the BBC were no longer able to guarantee job security as, like Tony in *Racing Demon*, they formulated plans to become more efficient in the market-place economy that the government was legislating into existence. Characters like Lionel, Donald and Harry seemed increasingly anachronistic. At this turn of events in the play, the largely middle-class audiences recognized in *Racing Demon* far more than a satire on the Church of England.

Act Two begins with a remarkable scene in the Savoy Hotel. Tony has been invited to dinner with the Bishop in order to discuss the future of the parish. Before the Bishop's arrival, Donald and Harry hijack Tony outside the Grill Room: they know he will be critical of Lionel at the meeting. Donald begins to read the menu. 'I'd have half a dozen oysters. And follow it up with Chateaubriand. Call it a Last Supper.' He then summons the waiter and orders three Tequila Sunrises ('with cherries and umbrellas') while the forthcoming meal is discussed. When asked to pay for the drinks, Donald starts to count his small change: 'Let me see, pieces of silver, twenty-eight, twenty-nine, thirty . . .' Imagery from the Last Supper is mixed with high theological debate and low drunken comedy. The arrival of the Bishop sweeping imperiously into the hotel ends the scene on a high note of suspense. Tony is told that he now belongs to the 'Savoy School of Theology'. But, behind the jokes, we sense that Lionel's friends are not going to win the day. They are the uninvited guests. The Bishop will not be on the side of the old order.

It turns out that the Bishop has been determined to get rid of Lionel from the start. In a final confrontation on the very day that the Church agrees to admit women priests, he vents his fury at Lionel: 'You bring it on yourselves. All of you. Modernists. You make all these changes. You force all these issues. The remarriage of clergy. The recognition of homosexual love. New Bibles. New services. You alter the form. You dismantle the beliefs . . . You drain religion of religion . . . and then you affect astonishment when some of us suddenly say no.' Although the Bishop is revealed as a machiavellian servant of the Church hierarchy, many in the audience at the National will have sympathized with at least some of these views. Richard Pasco, who brought the Bishop to life in *Racing Demon*, went on to play the only slightly more forgiving role of Malcolm Pryce, the shadow cabinet's Chancellor, in *The Absence of War*. In that play several of Pryce's accusations against the failed Labour leader echo the Bishop of Southwark's fury at liberals like Lionel Epsy: 'You are the reason the whole Church is dying. Immobile. Wracked. Turned inward. Caught in a cycle of decline. Your personal integrity your only concern. Incapable of reaching out. A great vacillating pea-green half-set jelly.' Hare gives equal weight to right-wing anger and left-wing vacillation in both plays. It is the human drama behind the conflicts that makes such scenes so interesting. Much of what the Bishop is telling Lionel about himself is true.

The second part of the trilogy, *Murmuring Judges*, has far fewer memorable scenes. Although Hare writes entertainingly about the barristers at the top of the tree, there is less surprise or excitement about the case of injustice he describes at the bottom. This is the one play in the trilogy where you begin to hear the research and, unusually in a Hare play, some of the characters do speak like interviewees rather than rounded fictional characters. Surprisingly, *Murmuring Judges* was received much more warmly than its successor, *The Absence of War*. In my view the latter is the finest political play of the past fifteen years. It is well known that Hare based it on his experiences of following Neil Kinnock's unsuccessful election campaign of 1992 when the playwright was given unique access to the Labour leader's war cabinet. This is part of the reason why the play has been judged as a documentary rather than as dramatic fiction. I saw it twice in a hushed auditorium at the Olivier. At the end of both performances many in the rows around me were in tears. But, reading the reviews and hearing people talk about the play at parties afterwards, you'd never guess that this had been the response. 'Why do the good always fight among themselves?' asks Lionel in *Racing Demon*. It is a question that *The Absence of War* raises and then answers in a most unexpected way.

Metaphors of war occur frequently in the plays of David Hare. Two of his best-known works – *Licking Hitler* and *Plenty* – are set during the Second World War. High finance becomes a kind of substitute for war in *Knuckle* ('the casual cruelty of each day'), while the heroines of *Slag* get up to some ugly manoeuvres on the hockey pitch at Brackenhurst. Class war forms the backdrop to *Teeth 'n' Smiles* and *Fanshen*, both produced in 1973. His 1995 adaptation of *Mother Courage* highlights Brecht's fascination with both the allure and disgrace of war. As the Sergeant says in Hare's rendition of the opening scene: 'They haven't had a war here for such a long time. Without a good war, where do you get your moral standards from? Everything goes to pot in peacetime.' Andrew Buchan, in *The Absence of War*, shares a kinship with Brecht's Sergeant: 'I have a theory. People of my age, we did not fight in a war. If you fight in a war, you have some sense of personal worth.'

Yet Hare himself is the product of peacetime, and the theme of his greatest political play to date is the absence rather than the presence of armed combat or struggle. At the start of the play Labour leader George Jones has gone missing before Prime Minister's Question Time. His closely knit group of advisers are kitted out with mobile phones and timetables, but George has somehow evaded them. It emerges that he went out for some tobacco – although not allowed to smoke in public – and chose to go for a walk in the park. When John Thaw's George came on stage at the Olivier, doubts about his whereabouts were still in the air. He entered quietly, with a smile of confidence, but also clearly amused by the panic he had caused. The playwright skilfully engineers an unexpected entrance, making sure our eyes never stray from his lead character. Although George is clearly adored by his team, he's also someone capable of stepping out, legging it to a park – standing and watching the action from the outside. He loves the theatre, which Oliver, his closest adviser, regards as his fatal flaw. George does spend his opening moments on stage as an observer. He leans back on a desk observing his team discussing the latest crises with an ironic glint in his eyes. He also provokes Oliver by referring to the tent scene in *Julius Caesar*: 'There's a scene in a tent. Before battle. All leaders have them. In plays, the leader always has a quiet crisis.' Leaders, George continues, always end up 'by murdering their doubts'. 'Thank God for that,' snaps Oliver. In this way, George's entrance is linked to a comic flaw in his character with a potential tragic outcome. For George is experiencing a quiet crisis that in the final scenes of the play will explode into a much larger one. In order to win the election victory that both he and his team are planning, he has had to suppress deep political convictions. We sense right from the start that George, unlike Brutus, has been unable to murder his doubts.

Oliver and his team have devised, they believe, a foolproof plan for beating the Tories. It is the blueprint for the campaign that led Tony Blair to his New Labour victory in 1997. As Oliver explains to Labour's new marketing chief in the play, Lindsay Fontaine: 'Elections, you see, people think they're about arguments . . . They think when politicians speak it's an act of sense. But it's not. It's an act of strategy. It's taking up a position. It isn't like debate. We're not actually debating . . . The only true analogy is with waging war.' George has already admitted to Lindsay: 'I'm afraid there's a sense in which I even quite like a war.' The old Labour rhetoric of class conflict and common ownership has had to be abandoned for the purposes of this war. George's speeches must not mention them. Neither can he mention the economy, which research has shown is the traditional vote-winning terrain of the Tories. At the first press conference of the election, an old Party veteran, Vera, lost in the new world of image-making and fudged soundbites, remembers a different time:

To hold things in common, this was our aim . . . Another
phrase: 'moral imperative'. This was the language of after the
war.

    Millions and millions of us. Most of us dead now. Went to
war and for the first time met the officer class. The result of
meeting them was returning to England and throwing them out.
In those days we thrived on discussion. To disagree meant you
were alive. Now it's taken as a sign of disloyalty. What is this
fear we have of it now?

This is the war that George has to remember but also to suppress. For the millions who voted for Vera's Labour Party after the
Second World War no longer exist. The Tories know who their
troops are, says George: 'They have the advantage over us. They
simply ask, what school did he go to? What bank did he work in?
Is he a QC?' In contrast the Labour Party has lost its armies:

It has no schools. It did have once. They were called unions.
But the communities that produced them have gone. The
industries have gone. So now justice recruits from the great
deracinated masses. The people from nowhere. Who have
nothing in common. Except what they say they believe in . . .
And that doesn't always end up being enough.

The Absence of War is a great political drama not because it
relies on the real-life experiences of Neil Kinnock for its impact
but because it makes a tragic hero out of George Jones. He is a
man of great understanding and humanity, and it is those very
qualities that lead to his downfall. During a television interview he
arrives unprepared for a question on mortgage tax relief and starts
to falter, presenting another fatal image to spectators of a Labour
leader coming unstuck on the economy. He has managed to flatter
the interviewer Linus Frank about his diet but has forgotten the
new rules of the war in which he is engaged. He ignored the notes
he was given by Oliver before the interview warning him about a
particular line of questioning. Getting such details wrong can be
fatal for a modern politician. The apparently united Labour Party

team starts to break apart. As a result, George requests a meeting with his number two, Malcolm, to ask for greater support in the campaign.

The two men debate the outcome of the election in an aircraft hangar. An audience watching this scene knew that Neil Kinnock and his Party lost the General Election of 1992, yet they were wholly gripped by the passions and arguments taking place on the stage. We were watching two characters locking horns over some of the great issues of our time. Our involvement was through the art of a dramatist, not a reporter. Both men respect each other. They begin nervously trying out various jokes. Then George starts to ask for Malcolm's loyalty: 'Well, yes. I mean in the past . . . you and I, Malcolm . . . we've joked about it. We've laughed at the Tories. Our jealousy of how they seem to do these things right . . . For them it's the great political imperative . . . You must always talk the leadership up.'

'We have tried, George,' replies Malcolm, as the audience warms to the humanity of the characters and begins to laugh. 'Have you?' replied George, a hint of a frown appearing on John Thaw's face on the Olivier stage, remarkable in that it was unaided by a television close-up. 'Certainly,' returned Richard Pasco's Malcolm with real sincerity. 'We have been trying. In every interview I mention your name. I always say: "This man is our leader."' It is not, of course, the reassurance George is looking for. But Malcolm means well. A literalist and Party faithful, he also fights his corner during the scene. He points out that George has lost the loyalty of the Party because he despises its elected MPs, preferring to spend time with Oliver and his unelected think-tank. George responds by saying that he is disliked because he brought the Party bad news: 'I shut down the fantasy factory. I told this Party it had to grow up. I made it contemplate reality. I told it to get serious or else it would remain unelectable. Do you think the MPs didn't hate me for that?'

There is a remarkable parallel to this scene in Episode Seven of Alan Bleasdale's television serial, *GBH*, where Michael Palin's Jim Nelson addresses his local Labour Party. In exposing the 'fantasy

factory' of the far-left, both characters are courting unpopularity
and charting new waters for contemporary British playwrights.
But, like Bleasdale, Hare is not a writer purely interested in political ideas. Malcolm defends his position by pointing to George's
real weakness: 'Very well. Everyone respects you. Everyone likes
you. No one will ever deny you've got guts. But finally, people
don't follow you. Because they know you can't cut it.' In spite of
George's secret admiration for war, he lacks a killer instinct. He
replies to Malcolm: 'Like all Labour leaders, I don't quake before
the enemy. It's friendly fire that destroys you. We all go down to
the shots from behind.'

Malcolm has won the argument. The flaw in the election has
been George himself. In spite of their doubts about George, says
Malcolm, the Party agreed to let him fight on. 'They said George
deserves this . . . He deserves one more shot at this thing. If you ask
me why, I would say our reasons are honourable. The Tories get rid
of their leaders when it's clear they might not win. But we hold on
to ours. I call that decency.' He moves in for the kill: 'It isn't the
Party. It's not that the Party don't believe in you, you know . . . I
say this in love. They smell that you don't believe in yourself.'

George now goes through the final test (he's nicknamed Pilgrim
by his team). His final speech at the election will be unbound by
restrictions. This is the one time when his old passions will be
allowed free rein. He will speak to the people 'from the heart',
with belief in himself: 'Without notes, that's right. On the backs of
envelopes. Like a Quaker, I simply stood up . . . And when I stood
up the words always came.' As his faithful foot soldier Bryden
Thomas argues, when people ask the modern Labour Party the
time: 'We seem to answer, I don't know, what time would you like
it to be?'

So George goes on to make his final speech. Of course, the
words no longer come. The years of compromise have eroded his
beliefs; there is no longer a place for the old ideals in the new
Party. Ironically, George has been responsible for his own downfall. Thaw fumbled for an instant, fell silent and looked at his
audience in amazement. Then he bowed his head in shame and

started to read from the notes he had been handed on the public-sector borrowing requirement.

This wonderful theatrical moment, in which Thaw sends the bucket down into the well only to discover that it is empty, was perhaps one of the most underrated by early reviewers. It was interpreted as a further comment on Neil Kinnock's final days as Labour leader. But Hare lifts this debate to a different level. In one way George is a great leader and visionary. But, in attempting to win the war, he has forgotten the basis on which it has been fought. Being told to speak from the heart, he has nothing to say; his Party has become a pale echo of the enemy:

> There's nothing you can say. You can't say anything. You're not allowed to say anything. How can I say what I feel in my heart? . . . All those hours in hotel rooms working at speeches, drafting, re-drafting, polishing, changing every word and all you're doing is covering up for what's really gone wrong. What you know in your heart. What really happened . . . You once had the words. Now you don't.

George's failure to speak stands for more than mere political incompetence. Like a tragic hero, he has sown the seeds of his own destruction. He loses the election because in essence he no longer knows what his Party stands for. This is why audiences were so receptive to the play. They could relate George's tragedy to their own experiences of Britain today. Over the past decade many of our institutions have had to undergo reform in the manner of George Jones's Labour Party. The universities, the BBC, our schools, newspapers and hospitals have enthusiastically embraced the language of managerial politics and the market place. Audiences at the National are increasingly drawn from these pro-fessions. Unlike the journalists who reviewed it, they would have seen in *The Absence of War* a metaphor that went beyond the everyday reality of parliamentary politics. George's inability to speak was a poignant metaphor of their own possible compro-mises and silence in the face of change.

During the 1970s David Hare became known as a writer who

created strong roles for women. In contrast to many of his contemporaries, his most memorable scenes were often given to
actresses. This is certainly true of his all-women first play, *Slag*,
and it became a notable feature of his work on stage with Kate
Nelligan in both *Knuckle* and *Plenty*, as well as two television
films in which Nelligan also featured strongly: *Licking Hitler* and
Dreams of Leaving. Helen Mirren, of course, led the rock-'n'-roll
band at the Cambridge May Ball in the Royal Court hit *Teeth 'n'
Smiles*. But it is less frequently noted that his most popular work
has often given equal rights to the men. *Racing Demon* is dominated by male vicars, as is *The Absence of War* by male politicians.
Bill Paterson's proletarian Archie Maclean was more than an equal
to Nelligan's upper-class Anna in *Licking Hitler*. It may be due to
his reputation as a political playwright that Hare's unique dramatic insight into the war between the sexes has been overlooked.
But the relationship between men and women has been as large a
subject in his work as politics. Often the two preoccupations are
linked: the women react to the appalling nature of men's lives.
Nowhere is this truer than in Jenny's account of life in the com-
muter paradise of Guildford in *Knuckle*:

> Young women in Guildford must expect to be threatened. Men
> here lead ugly lives and girls are the only touchstones left . . . I
> have twice been attacked at the country club, the man in the
> house opposite has a telephoto lens, my breasts are often
> touched on commuter trains . . . the doctor says he needs to
> undress me completely to vaccinate my arm, men often spill
> drinks in my lap . . . I have been offered drinks, money, social
> advancement and once an editorial position on the *Financial
> Times*.

Although this is a relatively early and satirical work, Jenny's situation is not untypical of Hare's middle-class heroines. They are
propositioned in the most bizarre circumstances, often proposed
to by men fleeing from the ugliness of their jobs. Yet a curious
sense of romance still prevails. In *Licking Hitler* Anna is seduced
and then betrayed by Archie Maclean in the most brutal manner.

At the end of her life, however, she is able to write to him about their affair: 'I loved you then and I love you now. For thirty years you have been the beat of my heart. Please, please tell me it is the same for you.' Of course, Archie does not reply. Hare's work also reveals a fascination with those who make a choice between working inside or outside the system. Often the distinction lies between being a man or a woman.

Skylight opened at the Cottesloe in 1995, transferred to Wyndham's the following year, and later to Broadway. It is essentially a two-hander in which a middle-aged man grieving over the death of his wife visits an ex-girlfriend to renew their relationship. Yet many of the themes observed in Hare's public plays dealing with the nature of political power and its absence return with remarkable force. Kyra Hollis has withdrawn from the glamorous world in which her successful ex-lover Tom thrives as a businessman and owner of restaurants. She now earns her living teaching at a tough inner-city comprehensive school and lives on her own in a primitive North London flat heated by a single electric fire. It is into these surroundings that Tom bursts one winter's night in order to win her back. As his chauffeur Frank waits outside, Tom, dressed in a highly fashionable coat, patrols the room. In the original production Michael Gambon's Tom restlessly paced the worn carpet, trying to contain both excitement and anger, his face and words registering shock and amusement at the conditions in which Kyra has chosen to live. Lia Williams's Kyra observed him calmly yet obviously in a state of shock. Caught in his furious headlights, she can only stare back like a rabbit. She suggests he take off his coat and he replies with cruel sarcasm: 'Well, I would. Of course. If you'd get central heating. Then of course I'd take off my coat. But since you've made a style choice to live in Outer Siberia, I think for the moment I'll keep my coat on.'

He does so for the whole of the first act. Immediately, we laugh and begin to respond to the humanity of this seeming monster. He launches into a tirade about the state of his business and the new managerial culture. He tells Kyra that he despises the bank manager and executives who now run his empire. Like Marion in *The*

Secret Rapture, Tom looks back at the 1980s as a creative epoch:

> For once you could feel the current running your way. You
> walked into a bank, you went in there, you had an idea. In.
> Money. Thank you. Out. Bang! They gave you the money! It
> was like for a moment we all had a vision, it was a kind of a
> heavenly vision . . . And then of course everything slipped back
> to normal.

Kyra of course does not share this vision; in fact she has chosen
to join the other side. 'You only have to say the words "social
worker" . . . "probation officer" . . . "counsellor",' she remarks,
'for everyone in this country to sneer.' She despises the new 'self-
pity of the rich'. But, although much of the play appears to be a
debate about Tom and Kyra's opposing ways of life, its real dramatic impact lies elsewhere. As in any good piece of theatre, we
witness a clash between two rights. During the first act of *Skylight*
Tom seduces the audience as he does Kyra. He is witty, energetic,
engaging; a man with a guilty and broken heart. He charms us in
spite of his hardline opinions. When Kyra expresses disgust at the
way he has left his driver Frank waiting outside, he pounces:

> For God's sake, Kyra, the man is a driver. That's what he does.
> You know full well that drivers don't drive. The greater part of
> their lives they spend waiting . . . Frank, as it happens, is per-
> fectly happy. Frank for a start is bloody well paid. He is sitting
> in a spacious limousine listening to Kiss 100 and reading what
> is politely called a 'men's interest' magazine.

Tom goes on to rage against Kyra's self-righteousness:

> These stupid gestures, nothing to do with what people might
> want. They want to be treated . . . respected like adults for the
> job they are paid for, and not looked down on as if they were
> chronically disabled, as if they somehow need *help* all the time
> . . . You could never accept the nature of business. I mean,
> finally that's why you had to leave.

Tom is triumphant but Kyra remains calm. Quietly she reminds him that her real reason for leaving was because 'your wife discovered I'd been sleeping with you for over six years'. It is Kyra who now brings him down to earth. Though he has invited her out for 'proper dinner', she resists. But she now begins to prepare a spaghetti sauce and asks him to grate the cheese. He complains about the state of the cheese but is clearly delighted by her gesture which allows him to stay – though of course he is unable to admit it. In Richard Eyre's production at the Cottesloe, the sauce was actually prepared by Kyra and the spaghetti boiled. By the time they sit down to eat the meal Tom has described the death of his wife. Though desperately guilty, he explains: 'I kept on saying, if I behave well, if I get through this, then maybe Kyra is going to come back.' Suddenly we are aware of two people desperately in love with each other in spite of their differences. As the first act ends, we realize they are going to sleep together. They go off to the bedroom before the meal can be eaten.

The second act begins in darkness with Kyra emerging from the bedroom in a nightdress. She searches for the pasta sauce, takes a piece of bread, sits down on an armchair with some schoolbooks to mark and begins to eat. Lia Williams found real sensuality and contentment in this moment. Soon Tom emerges, restless as ever, half-dressed and ready with some new proposals. He offers to take her to his house in the Caribbean for the Christmas holidays. She refuses to give a direct answer but begins to describe her new life in more detail. She describes her 'simple journey' to work each morning on the bus. It is not long before Tom has lost his temper once more. He does not believe she has found the contentment she describes: 'Kyra, in one thing you're different from everyone else in this part of town. You're the only person who has fought so hard to get into it, when everyone else is desperate to get out.' He is even more cruel about her concern for the poor and deprived: 'You're telling me how much you love the people! How much you're in love with the courage of the people on the bus. Yes, of course you love them. Because in three minutes you can get off.'

In some ways Tom wins the argument just as he loses the girl. It is true that Kyra's sense of commitment is part of an escape from

life, but she has found a peace in her retreat that completely eludes
Tom. The title of the play refers to the bedroom that Tom had built
for his wife Alice when he learned she was dying of cancer. The
bed had a direct view of a skylight at which she could gaze all day.
It was an expansive gesture that in fact brought no real illumina-
tion to the couple during Alice's final days and hours. In spite of
his generosity, Tom knows that he tried to buy his wife off with a
'perfect imitation' of life – in the words of another Tom at the end
of *The Secret Rapture*. The genuine skylight of the play is the view
from Kyra's flat. In the original production Kyra's uncomfortable
yet lived-in flat was framed by a vast window at the back over-
looking London. Here was a view of a London that Tom has forgotten; but inside is an emotional landscape that he tries and fails
to cross. As the couple review yet again the high points of their
time together – now knowing them to be over – Kyra reaches out
to Tom and admits that he is the love of her life. Gambon's pasty-
faced Tom, gazing hopelessly at his own ruin, barely hears her. He
rises, puts on his coat and a new smile, bravely saying his last
goodbye: 'At least, if nothing more, come to one of the restaurants.
There are one or two which are not really bad. I promise you, you
know, on a good night, it's almost as nice as eating at home.'

The ironies are several. In the course of an evening Tom has
missed his chance of finding a home. In contrast, Kyra has found a
home and is about to enjoy an unexpected and pleasurable meal
there. For *Skylight* is not quite a two-hander. There is a prologue
and epilogue in which Tom's teenage son Edward visits Kyra's flat.
In the opening scene he comes to tell her that his father is in a desperate way after Alice's death: he needs Kyra to talk to his father.
As he leaves, he asks her if she misses anything from his father's
world. She replies that she misses a good breakfast. In the final
scene of the play Edward returns to the flat with a breakfast tray
from the Ritz. He is in his gap year before university and has a
friend who works in the kitchen of the hotel. He lays the table and
serves breakfast – with the toast wrapped in napkins and fresh
croissants as she had requested earlier in the play. Though Kyra is
exhausted after her night with Tom and is now late for school, she

sits down with Edward and, reaffirming her need for some luxury, begins to eat. Hare's plays often include scenes where harsh and brutal decisions are taken about characters' lives before or after meals. Tom never sits down to eat with Kyra in *Skylight*. Yet its climax is probably Hare's most affirmative to date. Some semblance of family life is restored. The skylight has opened to receive the day.

The End of the Well-made Play

Skylight was David Hare's tenth successive play for the National Theatre. No other writer has been quite as consistent over the past decade. He has had an unbroken partnership with Richard Eyre as director and with both Hayden Griffiths and John Gunter as designers. Despite his reputation as a left-wing playwright, he has probably been responsible for many of the last well-made plays produced by the British theatre. Although much of his work is conceived on an epic scale, his characters develop in a way that is immediately recognizable to audiences weaned on Rattigan, Osborne, Pinter or Shaffer. The set and themes of *Skylight* transferred perfectly from the National's experimental Cottesloe to Wyndham's. In fact, as intelligent middlebrow entertainment *Skylight* was to have almost no rivals in the West End during 1996. Hare in this respect has travelled a very different path from the majority of his contemporaries. In the early 1980s it was still usual to regard the best new plays as the most political. The more serious critics often judged new work by what it told them about public rather than private lives. Hare's work was linked to a whole group of playwrights with whom he seemed to have much in common. Trevor Griffiths, David Edgar, Edward Bond, Howard Barker, John McGrath and Howard Brenton were all champions of public plays in large theatres. Unlike Hare, as the 1980s progressed, these writers fell increasingly silent. Once fashionable playwrights of the 1980s are now largely ignored. Why?

In the case of McGrath and Griffiths, the left-wing ideology that sustained them during the 1970s collapsed in the 1980s – both here and throughout Eastern Europe. It is almost as though they did not wish to confront or write about the shift to the right among the working class. They were certainly unable to deal with the rise of Thatcherism and the market place in a way that engaged the audience. Hare's *The Absence of War* and Bleasdale's *GBH* remain the only two works of the period that directly confront the unpopularity of the left – in a manner that had many of the critics suggesting that the writers had actually decamped to the Conservatives. The flight of Howard Barker and Edward Bond into historical fantasy also suggests a need to escape from the uncomfortable burden of reporting on the present. Nevertheless, it would be misleading to suggest that the decline of the public play has been merely a question of political ideology. The truth is that political plays have never been particularly popular with audiences. Liberal reviewers who pretend that there is a huge constituency for plays about the poll tax or racism in the inner cities in some ways do the theatre a greater disservice than their opponents who promote Lloyd Webber or the latest Coward revival. Curiously, it is often a writer's disregard for the importance of the values inherent in the well-made play – the consistency of character development and a well-heeled narrative – that lets an audience down. It is therefore instructive to examine the work of three writers who have continued to address public themes, but in choosing to do so they have opted out of the conventions of the well-made play.

The Politics of Style – Howard Brenton, David Edgar and Caryl Churchill

No writer has maintained a stronger opposition to the well-made play than Howard Brenton. He once compared the acts of a play to disparate and unconnected tracks on a long-playing record or CD. Throughout the 1980s Brenton became something of a lone prophet in the post-Thatcherite theatrical wildnerness. Continuing to proclaim the need for socialist Utopias to audiences increasingly reluctant to listen, Brenton has himself written wittily and movingly about his self-acknowledged position as the UK's most unfashionable playwright in a collection of essays, *Hot Irons*, published in 1995.

Brenton came to prominence in the late 1960s with fringe plays like *Christie in Love* and *Revenge* (1969). His reputation was consolidated during the next decade with the success of *Magnificence* (1973), *The Churchill Play* (1974) and *Weapons of Happiness* (1976) at the National. But during the 1980s things started to go wrong. He began that decade promisingly – at least in terms of theatrical impact – with the notoriety of *The Romans in Britain* at the National Theatre. The play aroused Mrs Whitehouse's wrath and she chose to bring a prosecution under a section of the Sexual Offences Act, claiming that a scene which involved a Roman soldier sexually assaulting a Celt constituted a real rather than a staged act of obscenity. The case was dropped before it went to court but it meant that the play hit the headlines and became part of a debate about violence in the theatre.

In fact most of the violence in *The Romans in Britain* is conceived through the text as dialogue rather than as on-stage action. The first half effectively evokes a pagan world of fear, survival and invasion through a series of harsh and bitter encounters between Brenton's divided Celts. There is a masterly scene in which Julius Caesar, bored and disgusted by the invasion he is masterminding, appears with an historian in tow to make sure his witticisms are recorded correctly for posterity. Michael Bryant as Caesar – cold, brilliant and poisonous with toothache – created the most convincing character in the play. But at the end of the first half both Caesar and the Celts disappear to make way for a far less compelling tale that was set against the presence of British troops in Northern Ireland. Brenton enjoys this kind of effect. He likes to run completely different stories and time zones together in a play, shattering the illusion of creating consistent characters within a dramatic whole. A two-act play about Caesar in Britain could have been a triumph, but *The Romans in Britain* tried to encompass a great deal more: the fate of the Celts, modern parallels in Ireland, King Arthur as the UK's last truly democratic leader. The human drama was therefore overwhelmed by the surreal yet essentially schematic presentation of the ideas.

The flaw is even greater in Brenton's initially promising 1983 play for the Royal Court, *The Genius*. Like Brecht's *Galileo*, which Brenton successfully adapted for the National in 1980, *The Genius* is a parable about the consequences of scientific discovery. An American physicist hides out in a British university, terrified that his latest mathematical breakthrough will lead to the creation of even more powerful nuclear bombs. In a beautiful winter scene set on a campus in the Midlands, the scientist discovers the traces of his secret mathematical formula mapped out in the snow. Unknown to him there is another genius at the university. A young female student has come to the same formula through her love of pure mathematics. But nothing is completely pure in science: the two meet and have to make the choice between publishing their results or hiding from them. These scenes take place against the comic backdrop of a parochial university concerned with its own economic survival rather than the integrity of its scientists.

The play falls apart in its second half. Brenton opts once more for artistic sabotage, abandoning any consistency of character in his storytelling. Almost everyone turns out to be working for an evil political power of one kind or another. The vice-chancellor now seems to be in daily contact with the Home Office. An eccentric don on a bicycle is suddenly revealed to be on the payroll of the KGB. A Trotskyite undergraduate turns out to be working for MI5. Finally the scientist and student make their political stand – as did so many characters in Royal Court plays of the 1980s – by joining the protesters at Greenham Common. In contrast to Brecht's *Galileo*, where we genuinely believe that the power of the Pope is threatened by the invention of the telescope, in *The Genius* political power is described in a merely fantastic and therefore scarcely believable manner. Britain survives, we are told, as a police state in which a mysterious establishment rules all our lives. This aspect of Brenton's work is best characterized in *The Genius* by what happens to Graham Hay, the university bursar. His wife has an affair with the American scientist and so poor Graham is dragged away by MI5 for questioning. He returns terrified and angry: 'No, don't touch me! I am holy. Member of a holy band. Who have been canonized to the sainthood of our times – those who have been in the hands of the secret police. English, but nevertheless, secret police.' The speech is ironic but also curiously affectionate about the English police state. Graham goes on to make an even more revealing remark: 'Know what? They're all old Etonians. It really is amazing to discover your country is a totalitarian state, run by old Etonians. In a big room with carpets and a fireplace.'

This sentiment has fuelled a great many political plays and television dramas in recent years. Joanne Whalley, who was the student in *The Genius*, went on to play the murdered daughter in Troy Kennedy Martin's six-part television drama, *Edge of Darkness*. In *The Genius* Graham hints that she may end up with a bullet in her back if she doesn't co-operate with the Secret Service. In *Edge of Darkness* she is murdered by the old Etonians for discovering uncomfortable truths about the plutonium industry. On television *A Very British Coup*, *GBH* and even *The Singing Detective* (in which Whalley again starred) fed on theories about an old-boy network of conspirators undermining the nation. Our most radical writers appear to enjoy the idea that their country is run by old Etonians. Yet the political reality of the past fifteen years is somewhat different. David Hare's work suggests that we are moving towards a managerial society which threatens the very existence of the old institutions so viciously defended by the Etonians in many other recent plays and drama series. After all, Mrs Thatcher filled her Cabinet with grammar-school boys, not old Etonians. At the very moment when the old Etonians were starting to lose power, dramatists like Brenton seized on them to explain away our political ills.

Brenton's best play of the 1980s was undoubtedly *Pravda*, which he co-wrote with David Hare. The play benefited immensely from having a central character who had a consistent role and did not change in wholly unbelievable or contrived ways throughout the play. Before *Pravda* (1985) Brenton had collaborated with David Hare on one other play, the 1973 Nottingham Playhouse hit, *Brassneck*. Like that play, *Pravda* occupies an epic canvas and deals with a heady entrepreneur on heat in the English market place. But, unlike *Brassneck*, Brenton and Hare wisely chose not to kill off their hero at the interval. As a result, Anthony Hopkins's colossal performance as Lambert Le Roux remains etched in the mind as one of the great 1980s landmarks. The play is set in the world of journalism and is clearly modelled on the rise of Rupert Murdoch and Robert Maxwell during the 1980s. Yet in *Pravda* there are no references to real newspapers or people. A whole array of fictional devices are employed to set the play at a distance from drama documentary.

From the moment that Hopkins's Le Roux prowls on to the stage, at a sportswear market in Frankfurt, we know that we are in secure dramatic hands. Le Roux is a South African and Hopkins used the Afrikaan vowels like a surgeon's knife – defiantly arrogant, probing, cutting matters down to the bone. He observed his prey carefully before attacking, his malevolent eyes nodding like the killer shark's on which he based the performance. In the course of the play the British press and its workforce succumb to Le Roux with surprising haste. Having taken over London's lowest tabloid, the *Tide*, Le Roux now sizes up its most prestigious broadsheet, the *Victory*. Will he be allowed in, asks one character? Le Roux replies directly, as always: 'Let me in? Let me in? Moral feelings? They pass . . . What are they? Little chemical drops in the brain. A vague feeling of unease, like indigestion . . . then in the morning it's gone. You're there. You're the owner. You're a fact. People adjust. The unthinkable yesterday becomes the way of things.'

The richness of the writing creates a true stage monster. But, as with all great stage monsters, our response to Le Roux is ambiguous. Despite his evil ends, he does often seduce us – by his directness, his dark honesty and his role as an outsider taking on a pompous and self-deceiving English establishment. If the play were merely a political exposure of, say, the real Rupert Murdoch, it would have been a far less interesting event. The audience would have made up their minds about the drama before entering the theatre. There would have been a clear black-and-white judgement

of the main protagonist. The case of Lambert Le Roux is more
complex. When he does take over the *Victory* – clearly based on
the fate of *The Times* and the *Sunday Times* – Brenton and Hare
depart from a seminal conflict in recent journalistic history. Instead
of focusing on a real clash of principle (that between Harold Evans
and Murdoch, for instance, over the editorial direction of a great
newspaper), *Pravda* sets Le Roux against the *Victory*'s rather
ridiculous editor-in-chief, Elliot Fruit-Norton. The latter is a complete snob whose chief objection to Le Roux resides in the fact that
he 'doesn't belong to the intellectual first division'. Fruit-Norton
has driven the circulation of his newspaper into the ground by
writing obscure editorials for an élite readership of his own imagining. When Le Roux topples him, we cheer. Fruit-Norton goes on
to become the chairman of the National Greyhound Racetrack
Inspection Board and from there he organizes a stillborn coup
against Le Roux. On hearing this, Hopkins's Le Roux replied:
'He's a fool. A joke. Mickey Mouse has a Fruit-Norton watch.'
The laughter rang out loud and long during performances of
Pravda at the Olivier. But it always reached a peak at the Fruit-
Norton–Mickey Mouse gag. There are no tears for the British
establishment in *Pravda*. 'You are weak,' Le Roux points out,
'because you do not know what you believe.'

So *Pravda* is more than a simple comic parable about the
takeover of our newpapers by an evil outsider. It shows how easily
we succumbed. In the play the liberal journalist Andrew is seduced
by Le Roux's charm and job offers. On a whim he is promoted to
the editorship of the *Victory*; on another whim he is sacked. Yet he
ends up in the power of Le Roux, humiliated but in work. 'To
everyone I pose a question,' says Le Roux. 'I am the question,' he
adds. 'And what is the answer?' asks Andrew. At this point
Hopkins paused momentarily in his performance. His response
came slowly as a smile, yet his lips made no hint of an upwards
curve and his eyes did not cease staring malevolently at his victim.
'People like you,' he answered simply. Politically, it is the liberals
and intellectuals who are put on trial by Le Roux:

I come to this country to organize your lives. I do nothing.
People fall before me as if they had been waiting. Why should
I lift a gun? People disgrace themselves around me . . .
Editorial freedom. You never used it when you had it. It is fast
gone. Why should you deserve freedom any more?

This is a very different perspective from many political plays
which refused to acknowledge the real power and strength of the
right in the 1980s. *Pravda* did so and won the acclaim of huge
audiences as a result.

David Edgar was the first among our political playwrights to
tackle the disappointment that followed hard on earlier optimism
concerning the fall of the Berlin Wall in 1989. Yet his much-
praised and ingenious *Pentecost* (1994) shows similar flaws to
Brenton's *The Genius*. The first act surveys the chaos surrounding
the new nationalism of Eastern Europe. Oliver, an Englishman,
arrives at an abandoned church in an unnamed south-east
European country. He is an art historian and has come to assess
the potential of a medieval fresco recently discovered behind a
mural celebrating the communist revolution. This part of the play
is a witty and inventive encounter – almost on the lines of
Malcolm Bradbury's comic novel, *Rates of Exchange* – between
Oliver and the East Europeans, who are struggling to control the
destiny of the newly unearthed and potentially lucrative painting.

However, like Brenton before him, Edgar decides to fire a few
rounds of artistic shrapnel at his own creation during the second
act. The play breaks stylistically from the first half. As with the
entrance of the British army in *The Romans in Britain*, refugees
from all over Europe and the Middle East suddenly start to occupy
the stage after the interval. They take hostage the characters we
have met in the previous act and demand to become citizens of the
EEC. The play turns into a litany of their complaints. From the
Bosnian refugee, to the Palestinian terrorist, to the Kurdish peas-
ant in flight from Turkish nationalism, Edgar literally creates a
modern Babel where all injustices are spoken and none is listened
to. Yet the sense of a play – in which characters develop in a real-

istic yet unpredictable narrative – is disastrously lost. The case of each refugee has been immaculately researched and described, but the characters do not come alive in the writing or performance. Everyone in *Pentecost* – and this is in contrast to *The Genius* -is exactly what they seem and therefore finally uninteresting.

Edgar is of course an immensely sophisticated and intelligent writer. *Destiny* (1976) remains one of the seminal political plays of the past twenty years and the first to predict England's swing to the right. *Pentecost* won great praise from the critics and a great many prizes, including the Evening Standard Award for 1995. Yet few reviewers pointed out that the painting which is at the centre of the narrative during the first act becomes an almost forgotten item by the end of the play. Oliver postulates that the medieval fresco pre-dates the Renaissance's discovery of perspective and therefore the beginnings of respect for the artist as an individual. The pro-gramme even quotes Leonardo da Vinci on the subject: 'The pri-mary purpose of the painter is to make a plane surface display a body in relief, detached from the plane, and he who in that art most surpasses others deserves most praise.' But the irony is that we do not separate the characters in *Pentecost* from their 'plane'. The historical background and debate so dominate the drama that we begin to lose a sense of individual characterization or 'bodies in relief'. By evoking one of the key assets of Western art, David Edgar also seeks to ignore it. There is no one we really fall in love with or learn to hate in the play.

It is perhaps unsurprising that Mrs Thatcher should cast a long, though often unseen, shadow over several of the plays discussed here. Lambert Le Roux in *Pravda* does not invoke her name, though she is clearly an inspiration to him. To the liberal regime now in power in Edgar's *Pentecost* she is a heroine, having consis-tently spoken out against tyranny in Eastern Europe while many on the opposition benches were prepared to remain silent. In Caryl Churchill's *Top Girls* (1982) her name enters the pantheon of fem-inism in an unexpected manner. The play is largely set in an employment office for high-flying female executives of the 1980s. The three women who run the agency are infused with adrenalin from the 1980s enterprise culture. However, one of them turns out to have a sister bringing up a child in extreme poverty. In the last scene of the play the two sisters meet and it is revealed that the daughter is in reality the unwanted child of the executive. It is obvious that the high-flyer in the family has betrayed her roots by embracing, like Mrs Thatcher, a false feminism of the market place. Rather in the vein of Howard Brenton, Churchill departs from realism in her storytelling. The first act is a surreal dinner party in which Marlene, the female executive of the second act, meets some of the great female martyrs from fiction and history, including Chaucer's Patient Griselda, Japan's Lady Nijo and medieval Rome's Pope Joan. As Marlene downs her chilled white wine and attempts to philosophize with her new friends, we are as yet unaware that she is about to betray their cause in 1980s Britain. The structure here is far more satisfactory than in the case of Brenton or Edgar. An attractive reality is brought to the scene by the high comedy that occurs when the power-dressing Marlene persuades Patient Griselda to try the zabaglione or orders brandies all round for her feminist troupe. It is noticeable that Churchill introduces the element of surrealism at the start of the play. Unlike Brenton, whose work often changes gear in a disarming way halfway through an act, Churchill seems to be entirely in control of her invention. Characters from history and fiction are introduced as simply as the girls who turn up looking for work in Marlene's office. By the time we arrive at the end of the play, the straightforward naturalism of the scene between the two sisters is all the more powerful because of what has gone before. The same ability to weave ghost-like presences in and out of the everyday lives of women can be seen in Churchill's *The Skriker*, which was first staged at the National's Cottesloe in 1994. A whole underworld of spectres is conjured up on-stage as two teenage girls try to come to terms with an unwanted pregnancy.

'First woman prime minister. Terrifico. Aces. Right on.' Marlene's view of Mrs Thatcher in *Top Girls* would be shared by the heroine of Caryl Churchill's *Serious Money* (1987), a witty play in verse about the amorality of the Stock Market following the shock of the Big Bang. The main character is Scilla Todd, a woman who delights in working in the futures markets and dealing rooms of the City. However, when her crooked stockbroker brother is murdered, she decides to investigate. Her journey takes her deep into the corruption of international capital where drug-dealing plays a major role in financing the major markets. Yet at the end she is bought off by an American dealer. We never discover the name of the murderer. There is speculation that it was 'MI5 or the CIA'. So the play ends with another suggestion that the old Etonians, now admittedly in league with their American cousins, are running everything.

Top Girls and *Serious Money* found huge success with Royal Court audiences during the 1980s, both being regarded as definitive stage plays about the Thatcher years. *Serious Money* transferred to Wyndham's, where the final chorus of 'Five More Glorious Years' was greeted with loud applause by audiences from the City who were about to re-elect Mrs Thatcher's Party for a new term of office. Of course they saw the irony but, like *Pravda*, the play became – at least for part of the audience – a celebration as well as a critique of the greed of the 1980s.

From Public to Private

In his revealing introduction to a compilation of recent Bush Theatre plays, the departing artistic director Dominic Dromgoole writes:

> Although it's the last thing people would say of the Bush, it's actually more of a European than a British theatre, in the sense of its understanding of stories. Many theatres are crushed by the heavy hand of the twentieth-century British tradition . . . This is the theatre of thumping 'boys'-own' plots and big noisy messages.

Dromgoole goes on to say that a typical Bush play is 'more glancing, oblique, opaque . . . Life and truth matter more in the Bush than point or suspense.' This chapter has been about a theatre of 'thumping boys'-own plots' and 'big noisy messages', with the obvious exception of Caryl Churchill. But it has also been about plays – including Churchill's – that have suspense and point, and that attempt to engage an audience on an emotional level with the great concerns of the day. The plays in Dromgoole's collection do not address public issues or stylistic invention a great deal, but neither do they seem particularly 'European' in their presentation of character. Certainly, three of them – Lesley Bruce's clever *Keyboard Skills*, Catherine Johnson's vigorous *Boys Mean Business* and Tamsin Oglesby's chilling *Two Lips Indifferent Red* – seem to be very recognizable pieces of British fringe theatre today. Much of the characterization is indeed witty and truthful; but there is almost no narrative to carry the action. The denouement of *Keyboard Skills*, for instance, has a Tory politician confess that he was responsible for the death of his mistress in a terrorist bomb accident. It is intended to be the final nail in the coffin of his personality. However, because he is describing off-stage action in which we cannot be involved – we have never met the other woman – the climax seems like a simple device to end the play and we lose belief in the central character. Equally, the burning of a shed on a seaside promenade is practically the only piece of on-stage action in *Boys Mean Business*. The play takes place against the background of some acute observation of male–female relationships and new working-class poverty, but in the end we remember a sharp chamber piece for actors rather than a comment on our times.

This does not mean that all plays require vast amounts of on-stage action to succeed. Jonathan Harvey's *Beautiful Thing* – a Bush discovery – was a kind of gay update of Shelagh Delaney's 1950s hit, *A Taste of Honey* (in which a pregnant working-class girl poignantly befriends a homosexual). The comic power of *Beautiful Thing* stemmed entirely from its acutely observed insights into the reality of coming out on a council estate. Yet the actual structure of *Beautiful Thing* is even more anecdotal than *A Taste of Honey*. Certainly comparing the two plays as films, it is Tony Richardson's movie of the latter that takes us on the more moving and involving journey. The acceptance of gay characters by those around them is finally more sentimental in Harvey. His next major work was *Babies* (1994) at the Royal Court. Here the story of a gay schoolteacher who has to confront the parents of his pupils with his sexuality was overwhelmed by a plotline that took its cue from Harvey's love of television soap opera and situation comedy. The plot veers towards farce, with antagonistic scenes between neighbours that might well have been written for *Coronation Street*. Unlike Tony Kushner in *Angels in America* or Armistead Maupin in *Tales of the City*, Harvey appears uninterested in turning gayness into a real dramatic metaphor: in *Babies* one is frequently reminded of the humour of drag queen Lily Savage who was recently an entirely acceptable presenter on an ITV comedy special.

While the Bush has been encouraging writers to lower their public voices, the new regime at the Court has been cultivating a post-Thatcher brat-pack of writers in their early twenties who are undoubtedly in touch with the mood of young audiences. In Nick Grosso's *Peaches* (Theatre Upstairs, 1994), the anti-hero Frank announces to his friend Johnny: 'There's no point in being old and saying you lived a little, talking about the war – you gotta talk about *babes* when you're old, tell your grandkids all about it. Fuck the fucking war!' Frank's existence is entirely governed by his relations with 'babes'. The scenes wittily consist of him talking to one girl about another – and then cutting to him in the presence of the new girl. The play is an engaging round of male chat-up and eventual disappointment. Alongside Grosso, writers like Michael Wynne and Rebecca Prichard have been presenting audiences with some cool assessments of their contemporaries. Much of the writing focuses on the personal lives of the characters; their struggles to find love and understanding in a recession-hit Britain which seems to pay them little heed. In general the plays are strong on dialogue but have virtually no plots at all. Wynne's full-length *The Knocky* hinges on a device – the stealing of a medal – that probably would have been one of a number of storylines in a single half-hour episode of a television soap opera. It certainly cannot carry an entire evening in the theatre.

By comparison, the first generation of Royal Court writers began with major rather than minor work. Perhaps because they had had experience of a World War and a Britain that was beginning to take notice of the young, writers like Osborne and Wesker could produce work on a much broader canvas. It isn't always the case that playwrights begin promisingly and then mature; sometimes it can work the other way around. It is disappointing, for instance, that Grosso's second play, *Sweetheart* (1996, Theatre Upstairs), repeats so exactly the dramatic pattern of the first. *Sweetheart* is set among the young who are in and out of work (the girls all seemingly employed by Channel 4), rather than the college students of *Peaches*, but the leading character, Charlie, like Frank before him, spends the entire play chatting up new girls. Many of the conversations are funny and engaging, but in the end the lack of any narrative or character development irritates. There is a moment when Ruby, one of the girls, mentions that her stepfather makes french windows. 'What's those?' asks Charlie disarmingly. He has obviously never sat through a play in the West End!

When the new writers do turn to narrative, the main influences often come from film and television. Jez Butterworth's feisty encounter with a 1950s Soho underworld, *Mojo* (1995, Royal Court), began life as a screenplay and is now being made into a film. One of the few new plays in recent years to be written with 'suspense and point' rather than out of a desire to describe a series of relationships, it caused shock waves at its première and won great acclaim for Butterworth. As an exercise in style, *Mojo* is breathtaking – evoking a gruesome society of its own imagining. The action unfolds exactly like a Tarantino thriller, with a group of tragicomic gangsters playing out the brutal consequences of a crime. The dialogue evokes David Mamet and Harold Pinter as well as Tarantino himself. It was a startling début that only begged the question of the point of it all. *Mojo* tells us nothing new about Soho in the 1950s. It is purely an effective location for a series of violent actions that delighted a predominantly young audience weaned on *Reservoir Dogs*. Its West End opening did not meet with quite the same critical acclaim as the first night in Sloane

Square. The fact that both *Beautiful Thing* and *Mojo* were originally conceived as film scripts rather than stage plays does suggest a change in priorities for the new generation of playwrights. From *Look Back in Anger* to *The Absence of War*, we have turned to the stage for entertaining plays that are also important commentaries on British society. That model seems increasingly irrelevant today. For the young writers of the 1990s, fame in television and particularly film seems a more attractive option than the theatre.

3 TV Drama – Small Screens, Small Minds

What do you expect, darling? After all, small screens, small minds . .
– Peggy Ramsay, literary agent, to a writer complaining about television

In December 1977 the BBC's David Rose held a press launch at Pebble Mill in Birmingham for his upcoming drama season. Rose had been in his job as Head of English Regions Drama for some seven years, his brief being to bring new writers and non-metropolitan subject matter to the small screen. Throughout that time the reputation of the department had grown, with the success of the half-hour new-writing strand, *Second City Firsts*, on BBC2 and a highly popular run of *Plays for Today* on BBC1, including David Rudkin's *Penda's Fen*, Peter Terson's *Shakespeare or Bust*, Willy Russell's *Our Day Out* and Mike Leigh's *Nuts in May*. Yet the journalists and freeloaders who decided to make the trip to the 1977 Midlands drama junket might well have drawn breath at the range and diversity of the new goods on offer. If, that is, any of them had actually got on a train to New Street station. The week before Christmas is not a good time for a drama launch in the regions and it is perhaps unsurprising that the event was poorly attended by Fleet Street. It was certainly ignored by the papers the following morning.

Two journalists who did make it to the December beano were the *Observer*'s fearless previewer W. Stephen Gilbert, who later that afternoon was actually offered a job in the department by Rose, and *Time Out*'s then TV editor John Wyver. Both were privileged to watch a preview tape that was to prove something of a landmark in British television drama. It began with extracts from the single plays that Rose had produced for BBC1 and BBC2 that year. The first was *Scully's New Year's Eve*, a taped studio play by Alan Bleasdale. This was Bleasdale's second play for television (his first, *Early to Bed*, had been a *Second City Firsts* some years earlier at Pebble Mill). *Scully* was based on the anti-hero of Bleasdale's successful novel about a Liverpudlian teenager, and his new year's exploits – transmitted by BBC1 on the evening of 31 December – gained a mixed critical response but an audience of over 10 million. Even more pertinently, Rose screened an extract from a Bleasdale work-in-progress for BBC2: the original one-off film of *The Black Stuff* (1978), directed by Jim Goddard, which created the characters that were to become a television legend in the next decade.

The second extract was from David Hare's *Licking Hitler*. The film was set in an English country house during the spring of 1941 where a counter-intelligence unit broadcasts black propaganda into Nazi Germany. Starring Kate Nelligan and Bill Paterson, the fifty-minute film was also a turning point in television drama, not simply because it was to win the BAFTA award for the best single play of the year. What marked it out was that Rose encouraged Hare to direct as well as write *Licking Hitler*. Although the locations were mainly interiors – and might easily have been achieved in a television studio on videotape – Hare insisted on using celluloid to create his vision of the past. *Licking Hitler* was transmitted in January 1978 to huge acclaim as 'a film by David Hare'. It was the first time a cinematic credit of this kind had been allowed by the BBC (previously Hare would have had to be content with 'written and directed by . . .'). This apparently minor alteration in a credit sequence was to have a huge impact over the following years: directors of television drama could now also become auteurs.

Other one-off highlights included in the pre-Christmas tape were Ron Hutchinson's *The Out of Town Boys* and Michael Abbensetts's *Black Christmas*. Hutchinson was to become best known for his 1980s Royal Court success, *Rat in the Skull* (revived in 1995 as part of the Royal Court 'Classics' season in the West End). Unlike Bleasdale and Hare, Hutchinson had not started his career in the theatre. His first plays were all produced by the television drama department at Pebble Mill. A script editor had read an unsolicited submission by Hutchinson who was working at the time as a National Insurance clerk in Coventry. Abbensetts's *Black Christmas*, beautifully directed by Stephen Frears, dealt with the ordinary lives of a family of West Indians attempting to celebrate a traditional Christmas in Birmingham. It was one of the first all-black dramas to have an impact on British television and the Guyanese-born Abbensetts went on to write *Empire Road*, the soap opera starring Norman Beaton, for the drama department at Pebble Mill.

At the time there was nothing unusual about the comparative lack of press interest in the event. Few journalists would have acknowledged Bleasdale, Hare or Frears as the likely key figures of their profession in the coming decade in any case. The assumption that the single play was the most important drama on television was unchallenged by the press or viewers. The BBC still produced around ninety new single plays a year, though five years earlier it had been 150. Unlike today, there were no grounds for thinking that a drama launch might turn up a story for the news pages or that the nature of television was about to change. There was, however, one other drama in the launch tape which might have aroused comment from the sharper-witted scribes, had they been present, and that was the inclusion of a drama serial called *Gangsters*.

Gangsters was based on a successful *Play for Today* that had won the Pebble Mill drama department both audience acclaim and critical notoriety earlier in the decade. Directed on location by Philip Saville, the play dealt with illegal immigration and drug abuse in the inner city. The writer Philip Martin had spent three months in the drama department on a script editor's contract researching the as yet untitled play. The outcome was originally envisaged as BBC Birmingham's first real contribution to the social conscience of *Play for Today* – a drama firmly within the tradition of *Cathy Come Home*. The latter was the first film to be produced by Tony Garnett and directed by Ken Loach for the BBC in the early 1960s. Shot on location, it provided the single play on television with its basic house style for the next ten years: documentary realism. Yet when Philip Martin and his producer Barry Hanson began to explore the night clubs, ethnic communities and gambling dens of the new Birmingham, they decided to abandon the grainy realism of Loach and Garnett for their film. Martin remembers sitting in a taxi with Hanson outside a notorious inner-city club and suddenly announcing, 'This is a town of gangsters.' The following day David Rose came up with his own suggestion that from certain camera angles the Birmingham skyline could be made to look like Chicago. A new kind of *Play for Today* was born on British television, one that owed more to Hollywood genres than the realism of Ken Loach. *Gangsters* is set among the night-time warring factions of Birmingham's multi-racial inner city. The Irish, West Indian and Pakistani gangsters play out their roles like Cagney, Bogart and Raft in the Warner Brother movies of the 1930s. The violence was blood-red, and a car chase that Saville directed around Spaghetti Junction threatened to outdo anything in *The French Connection*. Meanwhile the victims in the play – the illegal immigrants and addicts – found no help from the authorities or the hero of the film. There seemed to be no clear moral message in the underworld. Most of the critics were outraged. But the audience turned on in their millions – as they were to do for the two spin-off series.

It is only with hindsight, of course, that we can see the late 1970s as a watershed in television drama. The single play was to turn into the kind of cinematic film pioneered by Hare's *Licking Hitler* at Pebble Mill and further nurtured by David Rose at Channel 4 during the 1980s. *Gangsters* paved the way for a cycle of drama series in which the thriller became the dominant form. It dealt with a whole range of social issues – from immigration to drugs, from the IRA to the National Front – yet never at the expense of narrative excitement. There was a tongue-in-cheek quality to the dialogue and Martin even plundered the old Saturday morning serials for his cliff-hanging ends to the episodes. There is a direct line from Philip Martin's *Gangsters* to Troy Kennedy Martin's *Edge of Darkness*, Lynda La Plante's *Prime Suspect* and Jimmy McGovern's *Cracker*.

There have been important single plays on television during the past fifteen years. Jack Rosenthal's *The Knowledge* on ITV,

Alan Bennett's *An Englishman Abroad* and Charles Wood's *Tumbledown* for the BBC remain unforgettable achievements. But, rather like David Hare's plays for the National, they seem at the end rather than at the beginning of a line. *Tumbledown* was produced in 1988 and seems the last *Play for Today* that anyone can remember with respect. The BBC now produces a mere handful of single plays a year, the majority being developed for the *Screen Two* series which aims to compete with Channel 4's rather more adventurous feature-film policy. Nick Elliot at ITV's Network Centre has admitted publicly that a single play like *The Knowledge* could never find a place in today's ITV schedule. Since the early 1980s, therefore, our best writers have known that the highest profile on television comes from the drama serial rather than the single play.

Dennis Potter and the Drama Serial

The BBC season that began with *Scully's New Year's Eve*, *Licking Hitler* and *Gangsters* also saw the first transmission of Dennis Potter's six-part *Pennies From Heaven*, originating from an entirely different drama unit within the Corporation. Apart from his 1971 historical drama, *Casanova*, this was the first time that Potter had chosen to explore the television serial as the key outlet for his original writing. There had been precedents set during the 1970s, especially at Thames Television where Trevor Griffiths's *Bill Brand* and Howard Schuman's *Rock Follies* brought great prestige to Verity Lambert's drama department. *Rock Follies* in particular gained Potter's admiration during his stint as the television critic of the *Sunday Times*. Schuman's use of highly elaborate musical numbers to punctuate his narrative may well have been an influence on Potter's own work. But for many the opening scene of *Pennies From Heaven*, in which Bob Hoskins's sweetly sad and suburban Arthur mimes to the soundtrack of 'The Clouds Will Soon Roll By', is the real golden moment of television drama. Not only did Potter reinvent the rules – by clearly beginning a television serial in non-naturalistic terms – he also introduced the form to new ways of investigating character. For the use of popular music to counterpoint the drama of *Pennies From Heaven* inevitably brought a sense of past and present to each and every scene. Potter found a way of dramatizing memory on television that had eluded the majority of his contemporaries. In the theatre this had been the domain of Beckett and Pinter, whose characters are so menaced by the past that they cannot speak of it directly to others. The novel, of course, had been the traditional form for following a character through a whole lifetime: by summoning up the memories of things past, we find a link to the present day. But this had been the hardest effect for screenwriters to pull off. The use of 1930s song-and-dance in *Pennies*, 1940s ballads in *The Singing Detective* and finally 1950s rock-'n'-roll in *Lipstick On Your Collar* were Potter's key to unblocking memory and opening up personality, as the taste of his aunt's madeleine cake had been for Proust. We do see a Proustian effect in many Hollywood musicals. Whole communities and characters suddenly spring to life from the smallest provocation or detail of conversation. So, when Bob Hoskins's Arthur is out on the road singing along to 'Roll Along Prairie Moon', we are directly in touch with our memories of Gene Kelly opening the umbrella in *Singin' in the Rain*, or of Stanley Donen's three sailors leap-frogging into New York from their battle cruiser in *On the Town*. The overall tone of *Pennies From Heaven*, of course, is ironic. Arthur's hopeless and self-deceiving belief in blue skies leads him towards a murder sentence rather than true romance. But it is Arthur's enduring optimism and high spirits, however misguided, that make *Pennies From Heaven* one of Potter's best-loved works.

The Singing Detective (1986) masterfully employs every aspect of the serial form to create the equivalent of a true television novel. As with so many of the influential serials of the 1980s, we begin in the world of film noir. In the mist and dark of 1940s Limehouse by the Thames we follow a secret agent, Mark Binney, into a night club called Skinskapes where he meets both a British and Russian prostitute dressed in sailor suits. Suddenly we cut to a modern National Health hospital ward where we are introduced to the real

lead character, Philip Marlow, who is suffering from a hideous
skin disease. Michael Gambon's Marlow lies on his bed covered in
grotesque red blotches that are clearly visible from beneath his
pyjamas. His bandaged hands, swollen and contorted, are unable
to reach out to the paradise represented by the packet of cigarettes
on the bedside table. As with so many of the greatest performances, we notice the eyes first. They are constantly alert inside
his bloated features – watchful, flickering with anticipation, waiting for an opportunity to embarrass or hurt those around him. Yet
in contrast, say, to Anthony Hopkins's Lambert Le Roux in
Pravda, Marlow's eyes are not primarily those of a predator.
Gambon's eyes blink and stare in fear. Partly it is fear of his present condition. But Potter does not present the drama in a purely
depressing manner. It is not a documentary study of a dreadful disease. This hospital ward seems a familiar place to us from fiction.
We have seen aspects of it in countless plays and comedies over the
past thirty years. There are echoes of *Emergency Ward Ten*, Peter
Nichols's *The National Health* and even the *Carry On* films. The
male patients giggle over bed pans and the petty tyranny of the
uglier nurses – though never to their faces. The highlight of the
morning is the doctors' round or the tea trolley being wheeled in
by the nurses. Potter's Mr Hall sits upright in his bed trying to gain
his neighbour's attention, complaining that the tea trolley always
takes a right turn rather than a left towards his own bed. A
Pakistani called Ali lies in the bed next to Marlow, beaming at the
world while obviously understanding nothing of what is happening. Marlow himself faces the indignity of being rubbed down
with ointment each morning by the prettiest nurse on the ward. As
her rubber gloves move towards his groin area, Marlow desperately tries to avoid ejaculating into them. 'Think of something
really boring,' he says to himself: a speech by Ted Heath or one of
Bernard Levin's longer sentences in *The Times*. Or, better still, the
Guardian's women's page! It is to no avail, of course. Marlow is
forever being seduced by pretty Nurse Mills's eloquent hands – to
his supreme embarrassment.

During these opening scenes we are engaged by the pristine and

brightly lit comedy of Potter's writing. We sense that there are hor-
rors to come, but we are far more prepared to accept them because
of the comedy. This does not mean that the dramatist has delivered
comedy in the early scenes merely to sugar the pill of his hidden
and much darker subject matter. The hospital ward becomes a
kind of microcosm of the country, brilliantly observed and frequently with compassion. In spite of its immense complexities, *The
Singing Detective* is a popular piece of television drama. The audience will largely be made up of characters like those in its hospital
ward – middle England, bored, restless, frightened of death. Every
character in the ward shares Marlow's frightened eyes. They do
not want to know the truth. In front of the nurses and doctors they
behave like children and revel in being naughty. Ali wins Marlow's
friendship by bringing him a cigarette. In return Marlow shocks
the doctor on his rounds by saying that if Ali were to die there'd be
one less brown bugger left in the country to feed. Ali overhears this
and is delighted because the sense of comradeship that he shares
with Marlow outweighs any possible liberal anxiety about a racist
joke.

But Marlow's fearful state is not only concerned with his present condition. He is a writer of detective stories and has been
looking into his own past. The thriller that begins the serial is a
dramatized version of one of his novels called *The Singing
Detective*. It is pulp fiction of a 1940s kind. This world is peopled
with upper-class toffs and mysterious *femmes fatales*. His hero –
also called Marlow and also played by Gambon – brings a
Chandleresque edge to the kind of British paperback once penned
by writers like Peter Cheney and John Creasey. Into this mix Potter
stirs another ingredient. The fictional Marlow is a singing detective; based at a night club, he croons and swoons to some heated
yet overwhelmingly cool 1940s ballads. While singing 'Cruising
Down the River' at the microphone, he is able to work out the
intricacies of his latest case.

In the present-day hospital ward Marlow is also searching for
clues, re-creating the novel in his mind in order to find an explana-
tion for his illness. In the thriller the naked corpse of a beautiful

woman is dragged from the Thames and we recognize the Russian
prostitute from the opening sequence. Suddenly Potter whisks us
away to yet another time and place. The screen fills with green
trees: the birch, oak and elm of Potter's beloved Forest of Dean.
We return to the hospital ward and the ongoing thriller for a few
more scenes. The final shots of Episode One return to the Forest of
Dean. Here a small boy wearing 1940s short trousers sits high up
in a tree and addresses us directly. 'I'll find out,' he tells us. 'I'll find
out things . . . Who done it. When I grow up I'm going to be a
detective!' We have met the young singing detective.

   This is one of the most original openings in the history of television drama. It finds a link between a 1940s potboiler and a modern-day hospital ward. By the end of the episode it has arrived
somewhere else altogether. It is indeed a psychological thriller, with
the present-day Marlow in search of the secrets of the past. As a
young boy Marlow witnessed a desperate antagonism between his
mother and father. The father, a gentle, weak man, sang and whis-
tled memorably in the working men's club in the heart of the
Forest of Dean's mining community. His mother had an affair with
a man called Binney – his father's singing partner at the club – and
the young Philip has observed them making love in the forest. By
the end of Episode Six we have a complete picture of the man: his
relationships, career and the real meaning of his illness. We know
why he has chosen to write thrillers like *The Singing Detective*.

   The Singing Detective is also one of the few dramatic works of
recent years that have taken psychoanalysis seriously. At the start
of Episode Two Marlow is reluctantly put in a wheelchair and sent
to meet a psychotherapist, appropriately named Dr Gibbon. This
merely fuels his anger and resentment. In the spartan consulting
room Marlow sits like a brooding simian, unable to move his neck
muscles, while Dr Gibbon – gloriously played by a bearded Bill
Paterson – observes him from the corridor. Gambon's eyes grow
increasingly fearful as he starts to remember a scene from his
thriller. The sinister footsteps of an unknown killer are heard tap-
ping across Limehouse Wharf, slowly turning into Dr Gibbon's
own steps as he weaves into the consulting room to take Marlow

by surprise. The doctor holds a faded paperback of *The Singing Detective* in his hand. 'What's he got that for . . . what's going on?' asks Marlow in a feverish panic. Visually and dramatically, Marlow has become the focus of his own thriller. The victim rather than the murderer is at the centre of this television serial.

It is Gibbon who first notices that Marlow's love of pulp fiction feeds on an obsession with sex and violence that is rooted in his childhood. The prostitutes, hoods and songs which haunt his consciousness are there to protect Marlow from more painful remembrances. Gradually, childhood memories begin to dominate the serial – more mysterious, involving and evocative than the thrillers he once wrote. The narrative weaves through the episodes with a real sense of wonder. A London-bound train carries the young Philip away from his home, accompanied by his mother who neglects to tell him she has left his father. We are in the final months of the Second World War and the soldiers in the carriage wink and ogle at his mother's legs. Outside the window a scarecrow is glimpsed, reminding the boy of Hitler and someone else whom he cannot yet identify. Over the sequence we hear 'Paper Doll' being sung as we see Philip's father waving goodbye to him on the station platform – and then his mother suddenly running desperately towards him as a tube train rushes through a London underground tunnel. It is not, of course, the boy who is putting the past into this order: it is the man and the power of his mind. As the memories come back to him, Marlow's skin starts to clear.

The train returns at the start of the final episode. This time the young Philip is going home to his father in the Forest of Dean. In the hospital ward Gambon's Marlow has identified the corpse in the river, perhaps for the first time. The familiar scene from his novel is replayed as the police drag the naked woman from the dark river. This time it isn't the Russian spy or a prostitute, but his own mother. She ended up as a real corpse in the river in post-war London, committing suicide after being told by Philip that he has seen her 'shagging' Mr Binney in the forest. The young boy will carry his guilt across a lifetime, transposing his mother's death into pulp fiction as a grown-up. The boy goes back to the Forest of

Dean obviously changed. Walking home with his father, he runs
away and starts to spy on the perplexed middle-aged man from a
tree. He is now fearful of words, suspicious of his father's declaration of love, secretive and angry. 'Doosn't trust anybody again,' he
tells us. 'Doosn't give thy love. Hide in theeself.' A young detective, he has become the father of the man.

In the hospital ward Marlow thinks he has finally identified the
villain in his novel and also the identity of the scarecrow that he
saw from the train as a young boy. We return to the local village
school where the young Philip is one of the brightest children in
the class. The scarecrow is of course his old teacher who, as played
by Janet Henfrey, indeed turns into the most frightening presence.
'It has eyes,' says Marlow of the scarecrow. Henfrey's eyes survey
the children in her class like a hawk presiding over the sky. Clear-
sighted, cruel, working for a mysterious power whom she
describes as the Almighty, she casts terror into the hearts of her
pupils. Her investigation into the mysterious faeces that someone
has left on her desk is masterly. Her eyes transform the classroom
into a police state, turning over the guilt or innocence of each child
in a mere second. She engages the class in a terrifying prayer to
Almighty God who – she claims – will abandon running the
'whole world' for a moment to point down on the guilty child. Her
eyes glint in triumph, then slight disappointment as she sees her
favourite pupil in tears at his desk: Philip Marlow.

The themes of guilt and innocence – 'plenty of clues . . . no solu-
tions' – are woven as cleverly into the texture of the classroom
scenes as they are elsewhere in the serial. The schoolteacher is in
part a great detective and her cruel methods of interrogation rival
any torture that the hoods in Marlow's novel might invent. Young
Philip is indeed the perpetrator of the crime and, under the threat
of 'the big cane out of the big cupboard', he breaks down. By this
time the teacher has come to believe mistakenly that Philip is covering up for a friend. 'Who did it? Who?' she hisses into the weeping boy's ears. Philip suddenly realizes he can escape punishment
and his eyes circle the class in search of an appropriate victim. 'It
was . . .' he points, 'Mark Binney' – the son of the man who

'shagged' his mother and the name he was to give in later years to the sadistic villain of his first novel. It is after this revelation that Marlow is able to get up and walk for the first time since his illness, egged on by the irrepressible Dr Gibbon. To the background of 'Into Each Life Some Rain Must Fall', the two men fall into each other's arms, celebrating a miraculous cure that would not have been out of place in a Hollywood melodrama of the 1940s.

It is ironic that one of our most lauded television serials should have used the detective story as its central metaphor. The genre now dominates the output of both BBC1 and ITV in a way that could not have been imagined on *The Singing Detective*'s first transmission in the autumn of 1986. Yet the detectives who now dominate television drama are not investigators of themselves, but for the most part solvers of straightforward though increasingly gruesome crimes. There might be a place for Marlow's thriller on primetime television these days (there are worse ideas around than a singing detective), but controllers may now worry about some of the hospital-ward exchanges and the complexities of the flashbacks to childhood. Still, part of the attraction of writing for television is the challenge of engaging the interest of a mass audience on a mainstream channel. *The Singing Detective* held a primetime slot on BBC1 on Sunday night, having followed Alan Bleasdale's *The Monocled Mutineer*. Both *The Monocled Mutineer* and *The Singing Detective* won audiences of over 7 million, huge critical acclaim and an almost equal amount of notoriety. Potter undoubtedly relished the controversy that surrounded *The Singing Detective*. In particular, Episode Three became a subject of national debate and played an important part in placing the serial at the centre of public attention while it was still being transmitted. This was the one in which the young Philip Marlow sees his mother making love to Mr Binney in the woods. Details of the scene were leaked to the press, which did no harm, it should be said, to the ratings. Journalists began to create the figure of Dirty Den – or *Private Eye*'s 'whingeing playwright' – mocking the idea that anyone could be a moralist and popular television playwright at the same time.

In the end the Dirty Den image – pioneered by the *Sun* –

undoubtedly damaged Potter's reputation. But at the time of *The Singing Detective* he still seemed unassailable. Potter had delivered to a mass audience a challenging serial of a kind that had no parallel on ITV or even Channel 4. Together with *The Monocled Mutineer*, it was a triumph for the BBC and its drama department under Jonathan Powell's leadership. The brilliance of Jon Amiel's direction of all six episodes was acknowledged by the fact that he was never again to direct a television drama. Instead he went on to make a succession of movies in Hollywood.

After the ill-fated *Blackeyes* (1989) Potter's reputation went into a decline. Dirty Den was no longer a label confined to the tabloids. Accusations of voyeurism, megalomania and perversity were levelled at the writer who had insisted on directing the serial himself. Rather like a precocious film-school graduate – of the kind mocked mercilessly in *The Singing Detective* – Potter chose to direct the serial in wide shots without any close-ups. This left the editor with no opportunity to trim, cut or introduce a proper rhythm into the film, making it difficult to watch as well as hard to understand. In his posthumous *Karaoke* (1996), Potter actually makes fun of this process through the character of a film director played by Richard E. Grant. Like Potter with *Blackeyes*, Grant in *Karaoke* has directed a film that lingers lovingly on a favoured actress at the expense of the other actors. He finally understands that, in order to make a good film, he must first overcome his obsession with his leading lady rather than give into it. After *Blackeyes* few critics were to allow Potter a similar understanding of his craft. In particular, his 1993 serial for Channel 4, *Lipstick On Your Collar*, was notoriously underrated. According to W. Stephen Gilbert in his 1995 biography of Potter (*Fight & Kick & Bite*): 'The outcry over *Blackeyes* had a deplorable effect on Potter as a writer. He ran for cover and safety and tried to appeal to an old audience with familiar material and techniques.' The result, says Gilbert, whose view is by no means untypical, 'was a six-part serial that runs well nigh six hours and has nothing to say.'

The truth is that *Lipstick On Your Collar* marked a return to form by Potter. Both *Blackeyes* and his 1991 feature film, *Secret*

Friends, were dogged by narrative incoherence and a fatal absence of great comic characters. It is true that *Lipstick* relies on the songs being mimed in a way that does seem familiar after both *Pennies From Heaven* and *The Singing Detective*. But Potter was letting some sunshine back into his writing and storytelling. Starting in Whitehall in 1956, he weaves a masterly tapestry of romance and social comment around a crucial summer in post-war British history. Potter's War Office becomes the stage for some telling and entertaining comments on the class war. Here sit a group of officers trying to decipher material that has been smuggled out of the Soviet Union. The work is boring, repetitive and routine. Like the hospital ward in *The Singing Detective*, a little piece of England is placed in front of us. The officers bicker, argue and delight in provoking the privates who work as translators for them. The highlight of the morning – just as in the hospital ward – becomes the ritual of consuming the 'barely bloody drinkable' tea. Only gradually do the officers realize that they are monitoring the movement of the Russian army towards Egypt and the Suez Canal. As the war in Suez breaks out, so the cracks appear in the lives of the characters. The old loyalties and class rigidities are changing. This is why Potter chose to underpin the serial with rock-'n'-roll numbers. Here music is not a signal for calling back yesterday, but a ruthless harbinger of change.

The characters and theme are presented with a real lightness of being. During the opening sequences between the officers and privates, Potter draws on a whole series of classic British sit-coms from the 1950s, including *The Army Game* and *Bootsie and Snudge*. The War Office is brightly lit as in a Hollywood musical or in the style of most British movies of the 1950s. It is no coincidence that every episode of *Lipstick* begins in the crowded Odeon where Louise Germaine's Sylvia works as an usherette. Sylvia spends hours in front of the mirror each morning, making herself up to look like Diana Dors. She marches through the ranks of adoring men with the style and put-down charm of a Monroe or Russell in *Gentlemen Prefer Blondes*. There are very few graphic portraits of sex in *Lipstick*, yet the press still described it as one of Dirty Den's

naughtiest pieces. Undoubtedly part of the reason is the strength
and power of the role that Potter created for Germaine. The sexual
charm and appeal of *Lipstick* is due to its final note of celebration.
In an England tearing itself apart by the Suez crisis, the lack of
comprehension between the classes, the dark sexual secrets and
hypocrisies by which most of its citizens live, it is still possible for
romantic dreams to come true. Potter may not have won back the
critics with *Lipstick* but he certainly won back audiences.
Meanwhile the iconoclasm of the rock-'n'-roll numbers introduced his name to the young.

The vehemence of the critical response to *Lipstick* was partly
due to a frustration with the state of television drama. The writing
was on the wall for the old order at the BBC. The system that had
allowed Dennis Potter and his work to thrive through a creative
internal market was on the verge of breaking down. Heads of
departments and individual producers in the drama department at
the BBC were losing power. The new controllers and executives
were nervous of public controversy at a time when the BBC licence
was under review. Potter had severed his professional relationship
with his battle-worn producer at the BBC, Ken Trodd. After the
attacks on *Blackeyes*, Potter became angry over the fact that he did
not receive a single message of support from anyone inside the
BBC. So he jumped ship and went to work for Michael Grade at
Channel 4. As controller of BBC1 during the heady days of *The
Singing Detective*, Grade had been a great champion of Potter.
Undoubtedly, Potter suffered some distress over the move to
Channel 4. The BBC has been the most vital patron of writers that
this country has known; to lose someone of Potter's stature and
influence was a real embarrassment. At Channel 4 Potter became
his own producer on *Lipstick On Your Collar*, as Alan Bleasdale
had been some years earlier on *GBH*. This contributed further to
the myth that, without the expertise of the BBC to guide them,
even experienced writers such as Potter and Bleasdale can fall prey
to self-indulgence and become deaf to any criticism of their scripts.
As the commissioning editor for drama series at Channel 4, I can
vouch for the fact that this is simply not the case. But it is a com-

mon view held among journalists and independent producers, who sometimes resent large commissions being entrusted directly to writers.

In fact Potter was able to redeem his own reputation towards the end of his life. In a final and now almost legendary television interview with Melvyn Bragg, he announced to the world that his dying wish was to have his last works broadcast simultaneously by the BBC and Channel 4. He would hand over the responsibility for production to his own company, Whistling Gypsy. He would also bring back Ken Trodd into the fold to work with Potter's favoured director Renny Rye. *Karaoke* and *Cold Lazarus* were produced and broadcast in May 1996 precisely to Potter's instructions, as a unique tribute to the authority and power of the individual writer in British television. In these last two works the playwright shares with viewers his own sense of impending death. Like Potter, the hero Daniel Feeld is diagnosed as having terminal cancer. But unlike Potter, Feeld in *Karaoke* comes to terms with his fate as the leading character in a piece of fiction: a genre thriller that summons up the relationship between life and film, sexual attraction and love, and a final hospital bed from which the patient can no longer be made to sing. In *Cold Lazarus* the theme of memory has its final summation in a sci-fi future that depicts a society which has forgotten how to feel, yet able to find in the recollections coming from Daniel's head its most precious commodity. It is clear from the public's response that Potter's fictional memories are still important to them. Yet as Albert Finney's Daniel Feeld takes the microphone at the climax of *Karaoke* and starts to sing 'Pennies From Heaven' – miming to Bing Crosby – many will have been reminded of the unique role that Potter played in our television culture. He colonized certain areas and simply made them his own. Just how many writers in the future are likely to approach television drama with the same sense of vocation must be open to question.

The Bleasdale Trilogy

In Episode Four of *The Boys From the Blackstuff*, the beleaguered

Yosser Hughes enters a church after many years, we surmise, of
having been a lapsed Catholic. Abandoned by his wife, his job
long gone, the electricity disconnected, he patrols the streets with
his three vagrant children, still insisting he is someone important.
When the authorities threaten to deprive him of his children, he
can stand his life no longer. The priest is at first alarmed to hear
three children giggling outside the confession box as their unseen
father summons up the courage to speak. Yosser starts to breathe
heavily, then he begins to weep. The holy man cannot resist drawing back the curtain in the confessional to check whether he has
become the victim of a practical joker. One look at the death mask
that is Yosser Hughes's excuse for a face convinces Father Daniel
Thomas that the cry of help from outside is real. He introduces
himself to Yosser, even adding a little joke: 'Father Thomas . . .
doubting for short.' 'I'm Yosser Hughes,' comes the metallic reply.
'I'm desperate Father.' Warming to his earlier informality, the
priest offers a further concession. 'Call me Daniel . . . Dan.' Like
quicksilver, Yosser returns with: 'I'm desperate Dan.'

Non-readers of the *Dandy* will miss the reference to the legendary consumer of cow pies who is likely to have been a hero of
Yosser's childhood. Like many of Bleasdale's protagonists, Yosser
has thought himself part of a tragedy that is suddenly turning into
farce. 'I'm desperate Dan.' Yosser does not know whether to laugh
or cry at his own unintentional punchline, and neither does the
viewer. His solution is to headbang the confession box to pulp.
This characteristic physical response, combined with the refrain of
'Gizza job', turned Yosser Hughes into an even better-known figure than Desperate Dan during the 1980s. It gave Alan Bleasdale
the kind of status and authority on television previously allowed
only to David Mercer, Trevor Griffiths and of course Dennis Potter.

Although Bleasdale was obviously delighted by the success of
Blackstuff, he is far more reticent about the personal fame that
came with it. He does not enjoy the kind of public notoriety and
debate surrounding his work that Potter in his own way clearly
relished. Bleasdale often quotes with bewilderment the *Daily Mail*
editorial that appeared during the transmission of *The Monocled*

Mutineer, calling him a 'Marxist millionaire'. At the time he had an overdraft at the bank (no one earns a fortune by writing a drama series a year for television which, at the time of *Blackstuff*, would have paid around £1,000 an episode) and had not read a paragraph of *Das Kapital*. Yet, like Potter, Bleasdale has been a pioneer of the television novel. He has embraced the large canvas it offers, peopling his serials with a depth of characterization and narrative complexity that in another century would have been the cultural property of a Dickens or Hardy. Unlike Potter, however, he does not return to the same landscapes and situations in his work. In each of the three original serials he has written since the early 1980s – *The Boys From the Blackstuff*, *GBH* and *Jake's Progress* – Bleasdale has reinvented himself. The storytelling is always secure, yet entirely unpredictable.

What is fascinating about revisiting *The Boys From the Blackstuff* almost fifteen years after its first transmission is that it is not quite the serial people remember. Four of the five episodes were shot on single-camera videotape, so they actually look a bit like *Brookside* which was to adopt the same technical format a year later. *Brookside* has also borrowed many of the original *Blackstuff* actors, perhaps inevitably given the common Liverpudlian setting. The issue-led soap opera might also be seen to share common themes with the Bleasdale drama – particularly the impact of the 1980s recession on the city. But that is where any comparison ends. Five minutes into Episode One of *Blackstuff*, called 'Jobs for the Boys', and you are listening to a different kind of television music altogether. Unlike much of the political drama we watched during the 1980s and early 1990s, we instantly engage with the characters in *Blackstuff*. They are not mouthpieces for the views of the writer. They speak like real people and come to the small screen as fully rounded dramatic characters.

This is partly because they were first introduced to us in the one-off television film, *The Black Stuff*. More decisively, it is because Bleasdale endows them with real humanity and unpredictable dignity. When we first catch sight of Chrissie, Loggo and Dixie in tragicomic close-up as they sign on at the dole counter, there is

pride as well as fear in their eyes. Naturally they make jokes.
When asked about his present address, Tom Georgeson's deadpan
Dixie replies, 'The penthouse at the Holiday Inn,' while Alan
Igbon's Loggo claims to be residing in one of the better suites at
the Adelphi. Michael Angelis as Chrissie, the sad-eyed stoic of the
North West, clings to a fatal sense of decency in his replies. They
are all collecting the dole while earning a bit on the side through
the city's black economy. Bleasdale charts the scams and sub-
terfuges with wit and real energy. But his real emphasis is on the
boys' loss of dignity. Considered outlaws and even criminals by
the authorities, they refuse to abandon their leading roles as family breadwinners.

Dixie's appalling temporary night job as a security guard on the
docks is a case in point. He has simply been engaged as a front
man who has to turn a blind eye to the theft of a crateload of cigarettes. Terrified of the dockers' threats, humiliated by his own
incapacity to act, he returns to his family in the morning with a
growing sense that he has been criminalized. Dramatists have been
prone to forgive such actions on the part of their main characters
over the past few years. If women turn to prostitution to survive in
Kay Mellor's *Band of Gold* or a disillusioned socialist to serial
killing in *Cracker*, then surely it is because society is to blame.
Curiously, Bleasdale – who is often credited for having invented
this view in *Blackstuff* – does not go along with it in practice.
Georgeson's Dixie has every reason to excuse his actions – he has
to feed his family – but he cannot forgive himself. The disappointment and self-disgust are clear. Concerned that the authorities may
be on to him, his wife crawls through the house on her knees,
refusing to answer the door. Yet Dixie clings to a sense of order
and propriety in the growing chaos. He attempts to reason with
his wife and goes upstairs to drag his grown-up son out of bed.
'What is there to get up for?' is the response. Unknown to Dixie,
his second son is under the bed playing truant from school. The
focus on family breakdown becomes apparent.

The characters in *The Boys From the Blackstuff* engage us
partly because they have not entirely turned their backs on 'nor-

mal' family life. A sense of courage and indeed heroism remain an important part of their aspirations. The conflict between Chrissie and his wife Angie, played by Julie Walters, is at first seen against the background of the loss of a job. Angie wakes up one morning to find that there is no bread left on the table or money to buy any more. Bleasdale then begins to chart a wholly unexpected and purely emotional journey between husband and wife. Angie's anger with Chrissie has deeper roots than the dole. She has sacrificed her own ambitions for his; and he fails to recognize that his wife is his real support system. At the end of a long day of rows and recrimination, they fall fighting into each other's arms. 'Fight back, fight back,' blazes Angie, as Chrissie recoils from conflict just as he does outside the home. They look up to see their children watching on the staircase. 'Mummy and I are just playing wrestling,' announces Chrissie. 'Mummy's winning.'

Children as silent observers of family rows, husbands and wives clinging to their identities in a world where the roles are changing are as strongly present in *The Boys From the Blackstuff* as the dole queue or unemployment. Even the people who run the police-state type of investigations at the dole office are not presented as purely evil. Mrs Sutcliffe, the middle-aged spinster who runs the fraud office, is actually on the side of the offenders. Wittily observing the bureaucratic bullying going on around her, she delights in pointing out that without the unemployed 'most of us would be without a job'. Neatly and methodically she plots the downfall of her colleagues while saving both Loggo and Chrissie from having to face criminal charges. She examines character as well as evidence rather in the style of Bleasdale himself. The serial is therefore no mere black and white account of a social problem; it does not run on predictable lines. Characters suddenly reveal sides to themselves we never suspected even existed; there is a danger and tension in not knowing how it will all turn out.

In *Blackstuff* this is most clearly defined by Bernard Hill's performance as Yosser Hughes. Bleasdale writes his most important characters with specific actors in mind. Many of the original cast of *Blackstuff* were chosen because he had worked with them

before or had seen their promise in stage performances at the
Liverpool Everyman and Playhouse. Several – like Julie Walters,
Tom Georgeson, Andrew Schofield and David Ross – have had
major roles in all three of Bleasdale's original serials for television.
In this sense he has always been his own producer. When he witnessed Bernard Hill's powerful presence on stage, the actor
became the blueprint for writing the character of Yosser Hughes.
With the possible exception of Robert Lindsay's Michael Murray
in *GBH*, there has never been a more dangerous performance on
television. The other boys from the blackstuff cling to some semblance of normality in their lives, whereas the only wreckage
Yosser holds on to is a name. 'I'm Yosser Hughes.' Hill spoke the
line as a kind of deathly pagan chant until after a hundred repeti-
tions it broke over the city like thunder or the clash of cymbals at
a symphony's end. 'I'm Yosser Hughes. Everywhere I go . . . I get
recognized. Everybody knows me. Graeme Souness knows me.
I'm Yosser Hughes.' It is only the name that gives the man any
identity. The departure of his wife, rather than the loss of a job, is
what sets Yosser on his downward spiral. As he paces across the
city with three hungry children in tow, Yosser is no simple victim
of Mrs Thatcher's recession. 'Gizza a job' is issued as a demand
rather than a request. There are even echoes of Chaplin in *The
Great Dictator* in Hill's performance. 'I'd be all right if I had a
job.' But you know he wouldn't be. When he tries to cook for his
children, the kitchen ends up looking like an action painting.
Unlike Ken Loach's *Cathy Come Home*, when Yosser's children
are finally taken from him you also know that in his case the
authorities are in the right.

Hill gives Yosser a small moustache that seems to grow
throughout the serial. Starting out like a small prop in a silent
comedy, it has reached the length of Joe Stalin's familiar brush by
the end of Episode Five. Indeed there is a potential dictator in
Yosser Hughes. Yosser does not succeed in killing himself, though
he tries hard enough throughout Episode Four. He is there as a
ghost-like presence, haunting the streets and pubs to the end. The
final episode of *Blackstuff* charts the death and funeral of the

respected trade union leader, George Malone, played with huge dignity by Peter Kerrigan. George's last ride – the episode's title – consists of a final tour in a wheelchair of Liverpool's now deserted docklands. As Chrissie pushes his wheelchair across the desolate landscape, George starts to reminisce about the past. He remembers the days when Liverpool boasted the largest port in the world. He reminds Chrissie of the great battles that were fought by the unions on behalf of the dockers. Finally he asks him to help him out of the wheelchair so that he can take his last look at the port while standing upright. Chrissie struggles to get George on to his feet but eventually succeeds. George stares out to sea, clutching on to Chrissie. Tears form in his eyes as he begins speak: 'These dreams of long ago still give me hope and faith in my class.' He pauses as he utters his last words: 'I can't believe that there's no hope.' Finally he collapses and dies in the bewildered Chrissie's arms.

It was 'George's Last Ride' that fuelled Bleasdale's reputation as a hero of the left and enemy of the right. Yet the death of George in *The Boys From the Blackstuff* is a more complex dramatic moment than is often allowed. The old trade unionist's moving last words are spoken in a dying city – one that has been abandoned by capital and industry. The disillusioned and disaffected – whose ranks certainly include Yosser Hughes – will not turn to George Malone's humane brand of socialism for hope. In any case, Yosser is not looking for hope but revenge. The man who will serve him best in this respect is the Labour leader Bleasdale was to describe in his next great original television drama: namely Michael Murray.

GBH as a title stands for the Great British Holiday as well as Grievous Bodily Harm. The initials could also apply to the critical reaction that the opening episode caused among Bleasdale's left-wing supporters. For in his portrait of Michael Murray, the ruthless Labour leader of an unnamed northern town, they saw a betrayal of socialism. Yet Michael Murray is the true spiritual son and heir of Yosser Hughes. He takes the kind of revenge on his enemies of which Yosser could only dream. At the start of the first episode Murray storms into the office of his old headmaster. There

he confronts the man who once beat him mercilessly and sacks him
on the spot. He is then driven around town by his brother whom
he has humiliated by making his personal chauffeur. At a meeting
of the council later in the day he appoints his dustbin man as the
new Director of Education. Murray runs the city like a tyrant but
never fails to delight his followers on the extreme left of his party.
To celebrate his election his advisers persuade him to call a day of
action in the city. The turn-out is unanimous, with the exception of
a small primary school for mentally handicapped children which
has not been informed of the strike due to the drunkenness of the
new Director of Education. The headmaster, Jim Nelson (played
by Michael Palin), refuses to support the strike when ordered to do
so. Murray's troops descend on the building during the afternoon
in an attempt to drive the schoolchildren away. Banging on the
rooftop, dangling grotesquely from windows, calling for the
downfall of the Tory government, they terrorize both children and
teachers. It is against this background that Murray and Nelson
meet for the first time in the ten-part serial.

Murray strolls cockily into the school in search of the headmaster. His overcoat hung Mafia-style over his shoulders, he strides
purposefully and smilingly to the office with the headmaster's
plaque on the door. Here he raises a hand to knock, falters and
then moves away. The camera sinks down to the perspective of a
young boy – a six-year-old Michael Murray – outside the office of
his headmaster at primary school some thirty years earlier. This
door now opens to reveal a much younger headmaster than the
one he sacked at the start of the episode, but still recognizable. He
is accompanied by Murray's young mother. 'It wasn't me! It wasn't
me,' shouts the young boy, as we return to the present-day grown-
up Michael lurking in the corridor and trying to overcome his fear
of headmasters. Meanwhile Jim Nelson peers out of his office,
wondering why Murray has failed to knock on his door. He wan-
ders through the corridors and finally locates Murray playing bas-
ketball in the school gym, applauding himself for a particularly
skilful move. Nelson seizes the opportunity to order Murray off
the premises. Lindsay's Murray tries to exert his own kind of pres-

sure: 'Let me remind you, pal . . . you're supposed to be on my side, you're supposed to be a socialist.' Nelson raises his hand and Murray, not for the first time, flinches. Nelson begins to laugh and then turns serious. 'Don't ever use that word,' he hisses, with a strength and conviction audiences had not seen in Palin before. 'Don't ever, *ever* claim that what you are doing has anything at all to do with socialism.' Murray withdraws ungracefully, threatening Nelson with revenge. 'I know where you live!' he screams triumphantly on his exit from the gym. The assault on the school now begins.

The two men do not confront each other again until the final episode. By then both have travelled a long distance. What looked like a simple clash of good and evil has turned into something more complex. At times the whole weight of the 1980s seems to rest on the shoulders of these two men. Yet through the narrative our attitude to them begins to change. At first Jim Nelson seems powerless in his clash with Michael Murray. His heroism in the gym is contrasted by his private weaknesses and self-doubt. He is a chronic hypochondriac and has a fear of bridges. His phobias become stronger as he is harassed by Murray's henchmen. One night he ends up in the garden shed naked and weeping. He is like Philip Marlow in *The Singing Detective*, reluctantly undergoing psychoanalysis and having to face uncomfortable truths about the past. In contrast Michael Murray seems unhampered by doubts or inhibitions. Yet it is Murray who turns out to be the really damaged character in *GBH*. The incident of the beating in his primary school has scarred him for life. As a six-year-old boy, he was persuaded by a young girl in the playground to try and hang her with a scarf. When caught in the act he was caned brutally by the headmaster who – we learn later – was also attracted to Michael's mother. A mysterious woman called Barbara – in fact the dead girl's sister – returns to the city to seduce Michael Murray and destroy him. As the narrative opens and interweaves ever richer strands, it also turns out that a group of Murray's apparent supporters are in fact enemies and in league with the intelligence services. Murray has become the target of a right-wing plot to destroy

him and expose his loony-left policies. Stated so baldly, we might
be in the territory of a Howard Brenton conspiracy play such as
The Genius. The difference is that Bleasdale's drama unfolds as a
fascinating and unpredictable narrative over ten hours; and, even
more decisively, it has complete psychological credibility. As the
world conspires against Michael Murray, so our love for him paradoxically grows.

The flaw in Michael Murray's character starts with a tic.
Following on from this physical irritation, an arm seems to go out
of control and, as the pressure builds up, the loss of physical co-
ordination becomes complete. Few viewers will be able to forget
Robert Lindsay's performance in the hotel corridor in Episode Five
of *GBH*. In the bedroom his blonde seductress from the past –
played by Lindsay Duncan – waits on her bed. Outside Murray
tries to get his body into some kind of order. Harassing a
Rastafarian waiter who is bringing the champagne, he runs to hide
in the lift, ashamed at exposing his insanity to the new love of his
life. Inside the lift his arm rises and brings down a piece of the ceil-
ing. He falls to his knees as the waiter stops the lift door from closing and informs him that his wife is in the reception area of the
hotel: it might not be the perfect moment to descend to the ground
floor. Immediately Murray rushes out of the lift, begging the
waiter's forgiveness. He arrives at the bedroom door, condoms
tumbling from his pocket, knocks and crashes on to the carpet at
the feet of Lindsay Duncan's Barbara. 'Isn't he wonderful,' she
pronounces, closing the door on both waiter and viewer.

The scene owes a great deal to Robert Lindsay's comic timing
and flair for dramatic panic, even though the stage directions were
taken verbatim from Bleasdale's original script. But our involvement in the farce is a result of the tragedy that has preceded it.
The comedy is energized by our knowledge of Michael Murray's
past. It is interesting that *GBH* attracted an unusually young audience for a drama series. Whereas some critics were dismayed by
the introduction of comedy and even farce into a supposedly serious political drama, the television audience had no such problem.
In situation comedies like *The Young Ones*, *Blackadder* and

Absolutely Fabulous, there is an element of anarchy and absurdism which the young feel is an appropriate response to the world as they see it. Bleasdale is one of our few serious dramatists to capitalize on this. His stage plays contain many moments of high farce; but often we have not had time to get to know the characters on a realistic basis, so we only experience a black comedy. But just as *The Singing Detective* took us into the past of Philip Marlow, down the real mean streets of a man's private hell, so in *GBH* we come to know Michael Murray and his real motivation for becoming a Labour leader of the council. Like Potter, Bleasdale needs the epic canvas of a multi-layered television serial – including comic anarchy – to tell his stories properly.

Michael Murray's real tragedy is that he is motivated by revenge. His own father was a humane trade unionist – possibly like George Malone – who died before Michael could know him. Michael grew up seeking his mother's love and approval but never found it. The elderly Mrs Murray sits in her front room dazed by the past and unable to give her son the acknowledgement he craves. So the socialism he champions – like the machiavellian Trotskyites who befriend him – has its roots in personal vendetta rather than principle, anger rather than hope. In a bizarre manner it mirrors the right-wing power game that leads to his final downfall. Many people who saw in *The Boys From the Blackstuff* a simple endorsement of socialist values were horrified by the darker politics of *GBH*. Yet, like David Hare's *The Absence of War*, it remains one of the truer dramatic accounts of the Labour Party during the past decade.

Jim Nelson confronts Michael Murray again at a Labour Party meeting during the final episode of *GBH*. This time he completely wins the argument. Murray is about to be arrested for corruption; his tyranny has come unstuck, his fleeting hour of fame about to end. Rather like George Jones in *The Absence of War*, Jim Nelson argues for the middle ground. 'The further left you go,' he reasons, pointing at the defeated Murray, 'the more right-wing you become.' Like Jones, he declares that it is time to shut down the fantasy factory and begin a realistic appraisal of the Party's

chances of regaining power. But curiously enough, we do not thank
him for these home truths. For our emotional engagement is now
with Michael Murray. A good dramatist presents both sides of an
argument. A great dramatist can make an audience love and hate a
character at the same moment. This is what Bleasdale achieves in
GBH. Jim Nelson grows to maturity and strength just as we fall
out of love with him. The appalling Michael Murray wins our
affection at the moment when he loses power. For, like Yosser
Hughes, he is the more typical and damaged product of our age.

   GBH caused something of a political storm on its transmission
in the spring of 1991. Many were surprised by the fact that in his
next major work for television, *Jake's Progress* (1995), Bleasdale
seemed to lack any political profile. At first sight the story of Julie
and Jamie Diadoni and their son Jake is a purely domestic drama.
As in Ingmar Bergman's serial, *Scenes From a Marriage*, we witness a slow tortured breakdown of a family over several weeks –
though in Bleasdale's case the tone is always enlivened by dark
comedy. Admittedly, Jamie has lost his job four years before the
serial begins and Julie is struggling to keep the family going on her
income as a nurse. As the bank starts to foreclose on their mortgage, there are echoes of the beautifully orchestrated row between
Chrissie and Angie in *The Boys From the Blackstuff*. Indeed Julie
Walters played both Angie and Mrs Diadoni in the serials.
However, the real focus is on six-year-old Jake; it is through his
eyes that we observe a family crisis of the mid-1990s. Jake has
been effectively brought up by his father. It is Jamie who has taken
him to the playground, cooked his lunch and read to him at bed-
time. His mother comes home from work each evening looking
exhausted with a scowl on her face. The boy has interpreted these
signs to mean that his mother does not love him; and indeed Julie
does seem to treat Jake with despairing indifference at times. 'Play
with me, Daddy' is Jake's catchphrase – a cry that echoes with
touching and ferocious irony across the nine hours of the serial.

   From this apparently simple but actually complex beginning,
Bleasdale constructs a truly epic narrative. He does so by inter-
weaving three dramatic strands which unfold in an entirely unpre-

dictable but – at the final count – wholly inevitable manner. Firstly there is Jake's progress through the serial. An apparently content and well-loved child, he seethes with inner anger and confusion in front of both parents. When Julie becomes pregnant after an unprotected night of sex with Jamie, Jake starts to listen to his parents' rows behind the door. Against all expectations, Julie decides to have the baby. Her husband is pleased but as usual confused. 'Why?' he asks Julie, with Jake listening intently outside. 'Why do you want to have another child?' In tears, she answers: ' . . . because I want a better child than Jake.' The camera of course moves to Jake whose life is now changed for ever. He begins mentally to plan the demise of the new baby and possibly his whole family – with the single exception of his father. But first Jake tries and fails to hang himself on the clothes-line in the garden. When the baby is born, Jake sets to work on his highchair with a screwdriver. Seconds after Julie has taken the new baby in her arms, the highchair collapses. Later in the serial Jake dresses up as a Red Indian, puts his baby brother in a cowboy costume and tries to burn him at the stake. Though deeply shocking, these sequences are also richly comic. From Jake's point of view his actions are purely logical. His parents meanwhile have no idea that they have turned their blond, blue-eyed and beautiful young son into a potential murderer.

At every turn Jake's plans are thwarted by some unforeseen circumstance in the adult world. Many reviewers were disappointed that Jake failed to murder anyone (though they overlooked the fact that he was indirectly responsible for his grandfather's death through an ingenious piece of plotting by Bleasdale). They felt this might have made a more compelling narrative out of *Jake's Progress*. But such a turn of events would have been entirely out of keeping with the intentions of the serial. It is Bleasdale's genius to keep us involved and enthralled in his story by not resorting to the obvious or crudely exploitative. The serial is about the consequences of our actions: despite the best intentions, we send our children off on to the wrong paths. The real violence in the story happens elsewhere.

The second strand of the plotline involves Robert Lindsay's Jamie. Early on in the serial he has his palm read at a party. He is told by a friend and amateur fortune teller (played by Lindsay Duncan, the *femme fatale* in *GBH*) that before he dies he will have an affair. This has a profound effect on him. For the first time he realizes that he is not happy in his own marriage. He starts to look at the other mothers in Jake's playground with a different eye, now fantasizing about the women and yet thinking he might die as a result of actually sleeping with one of them. The viewer, of course, is waiting for an affair to happen. The arrival of a local farmhand's daughter signals the beginning of Jamie's end. She is in fact a murderess, a beautiful but dangerous woman, who immediately stalks Jamie as her prey. Through a series of hilarious, unpredictable and finally tragic events, Bleasdale shows us how the fortune teller's prophecy comes true. A lesser dramatist would have simply contrived Jamie's death at the hands of his lover. That is what Jamie fears. When he finally gets to embrace her in her cottage and remove her clothes, he hears the report of a gun. Lindsay's Jamie leaps out of his underpants in panic, thinking he has been shot. But, true to form, Bleasdale confounds our expectations. Jamie has not been shot. Outside the girl's bedroom door, her wretched and drunken father has committed suicide – watched from behind the sofa by Jake.

Jamie learns in the final episode that the fortune teller had been playing a trick on him at the party. His wife Julie is exposed as the real perpetrator of the crime; she suggested the joke in order to test his fidelity. It has rebounded on her dramatically. Jamie now feels free to begin an affair without guilt. The marriage is finally over. This is where Bleasdale's skill as a dramatist truly excels. The playground to which Jake goes overlooks the sea. With his father's departure, he visits it for the first time with his mother. Still calling out 'Play with me, Daddy!' on the swing, though being pushed by his mother, he suddenly observes two people on the clifftop. It is Jamie and his girlfriend. Jake is overjoyed. He jumps off the swing and promptly turns into an aeroplane, his arms extending towards the sky: a ritual he has enacted many times with Jamie. He runs furiously towards the edge of the cliff and into the arms of his father. Of course the impact sends three people over the edge – father, son and girlfriend – hurtling towards their deaths. In the air Jamie lets go of his girlfriend's hand and abandons her to fate. Instead he embraces his son in a desperate attempt to cushion him from the fall. Jamie crashes to his death on the beach but Jake survives the impact as he lands on his father's body. The prophecy has been fulfilled but not in the expected manner. Jake has been responsible for the one death in the family he did not wish to bring about.

The third strand of *Jake's Progress* is even more moving: the journey undertaken by Jamie's wife Julie. It is perhaps unfortunate that Bleasdale gave the character the same Christian name as his leading actress, for Julie Walters's performance as the wife in *Jake's Progress* is probably her best work for Bleasdale to date. She begins on a hard and even unsympathetic note. Less joyous than Jamie, exhausted by her struggle to make ends meet, she is equally stunned by the fact that she has lost her son's love. Yet whether she confronts her bank manager about selling the house ('But where will we *live*?') or her mother about her husband's uselessness, there is a flame of brightness about her performance. In the midst of a furious row with her husband, she flings an empty wine bottle at him and storms out, shouting: 'If you think this is a prelude to the best sex we've ever had you're *mistaken*!' This is hardly a common occurrence in marital rows on television. But it is Julie in *Jake's Progress* who also undertakes the challenge of finding out what has happened to her son. She has two unforgettable monologues in the serial. The first is in front of her mother who has fallen asleep on her bed. Here she confronts the fact that she can only remember one day in her life when her own mother played with her – something that has clearly affected her relationship with Jake. As Julie relives her only happy childhood memory, the actress brings the day alive. Through her words we conjure up the image of Julie as a young girl experiencing joy for the first time; and we know she is thinking of Jake as much as herself. The second monologue is in front of Jake in the final episode of the serial.

Here she sits in a corner bouncing a ball in front of the sulking child. Through persistence, humour and honesty, she tries to apologize to him. Parents, she tells Jake, will always love children more than children love parents. That is how it should be; that is how the world works. When Jake grows up he will love his children more than they do him. The ball continues to bounce. Jake looks up at his mother and catches it. She has started to win back his love. He almost smiles. After the terrible fall from the cliff at the end of the serial, Jake opens his eyes and sees the mother who has come to rescue him. Julie has witnessed the kind of tragedy that only a Medea or Hecuba could have done before her. 'Play with me, *Mummy*!' Jake says for the first time.

The Triumph of Genre

There is no question that, of the three original Bleasdale serials discussed above, *Jake's Progress* is the most surprising and in some ways the greater achievement. *The Boys From the Blackstuff* may have had a more devastating impact on society and television drama in general; *GBH* certainly caused a wider political controversy. But as an original television novel, based purely on family relationships, *Jake's Progress* has no precedent other than perhaps John Hopkins's powerful 1960s drama, *Talking To a Stranger*. *Jake* was no documentary case study of a disadvantaged child. Bleasdale was writing about what can go wrong in a 'normal' and even loving family. As a metaphor for Britain in the 1990s, it was both unexpected and extremely disturbing. Yet this is by no means the common perception about the serial or of Bleasdale's achievement in writing it. It is helpful for an understanding of television drama today to consider why.

Jake's Progress was transmitted during the autumn of 1995 on Channel 4 in a very different cultural climate from either *The Boys From the Blackstuff* or *GBH*. Watching *Blackstuff* today, you are reminded of a time when television drama was not dominated by the crime genre. The basic plot is confidently rooted in recognizable characters and credible dialogue. There is suspense and many of the scenes have a tension that is absent from the majority of today's cop shows. But Yosser, Chrissie and Loggo are part of a television culture that placed human drama at the centre of the storytelling. The speech patterns of the characters are based on the way people actually speak. This is certainly true of the great television thrillers of the 1980s and 1990s: Kennedy Martin's *Edge of Darkness*, La Plante's *Prime Suspect* and the early episodes of Jimmy McGovern's *Cracker*. It is no longer true of their successors or the vast majority of the drama shown on either ITV or BBC1.

The police series that now dominate our screens are plot-led and curiously characterless. The dialogue is entirely functional, there to provide information that is free from any worrying subtext. The stories are often copied from previously successful shows, particularly *Prime Suspect* and *Cracker*, which may explain a proliferation of serial rapists in the programmes that is totally out of proportion to their actual presence in the United Kingdom. The writers on the original *Z Cars* for the BBC in the 1960s were only allowed one murder every fifty episodes; the rest of the time they had to use their imaginations more creatively. I doubt whether the producers or writers of the new investigative shows would be able to fulfil such a brief. The new shows often need a sensational murder each week to keep viewers tuning in. The production values of the series are high. But on primetime television it often seems as though we are watching the same characters following the same killers, followed by the same lighting cameramen reading the same stage directions. It is rumoured that, when television actors meet each other in the BBC canteen these days, they no longer ask: 'What are you playing?' but 'What are you investigating?'

The majority of these series are not commissioned on the enthusiasm of a particular producer or drama head. Ever since ITV declared that the criterion for success had to be long-running drama series with ratings of over 10 million viewers, the rules of the television game began to change. New programme ideas are now concept-led and tested out on viewers before being commissioned. BBC1 has had to compete with ITV's past successes by ordering up a whole string of derivative police shows of its own. The loser in this process has undoubtedly been the viewer. When *Jake* was transmitted, it was the only television drama on air that was not rooted in a recognizable genre or safe formula, with the possible exception of *Pride and Prejudice*.

This chapter began with an account of a press launch organized in 1977 by a small section of the BBC's drama department. The Pebble Mill team was only one among many at the BBC at that time. Such a press launch would never take place today because autonomous departments with real power no longer exist within the BBC. The environment that led to Bleasdale joining forces with BBC producer Michael Wearing on *Blackstuff* or Potter with Ken Trodd on *Pennies From Heaven* has largely disappeared. Producers and script editors now work on short-term contracts, with any renewal being dependent on the success or otherwise of their latest programme. If Bleasdale and Potter had been judged by the response to their first plays on television – as they would undoubtedly be today – they would never have gone on to write *The Monocled Mutineer* or *The Singing Detective*. There is no right to fail in drama within the current BBC or ITV structures. Michael Wearing still has an office at the BBC, while Ken Trodd's phone was cut off in early 1997. Neither has a budget to be able to ensure that their enthusiasms reach the screen. For money they have to go bowl in hand like Oliver Twist to the controllers of BBC1 and BBC2, who will often seek their own advice before giving a decision. It took Wearing fourteen years of argument and perseverance before getting the green light for Peter Flannery's *Our Friends in the North* on BBC2. The latest reforms at the BBC make it unclear whether BBC drama producers will be left with any commissioning powers at all. In Dennis Potter's final work, *Cold Lazarus*, a group of scientists of the future watch with amazement the stories and scenes coming from writer Daniel Feeld's frozen head. They are watching the unfolding of a drama serial of a kind that is now unseen in their nevertheless entertainment-dominated society. Let us hope that the actual viewers of the future have easier access to the best imaginations.

4 Film – The Calling Card

> KYRA: It's the same with new films. I just won't go to them. Old
>   films I like.
> TOM: Ah. Those you like because they're romantic.
> KYRA: You can hardly deny it. They have something we don't.
>   – David Hare, *Skylight*

The writing of screenplays occupies a place in modern British culture that would have been unthinkable even a decade ago. It was the intervention of Channel 4 during the early 1980s, with its policy of showing television films in the cinema, that led to a completely new set of expectations on the part of our writers and directors. At the BBC the majority of single dramas were transmitted once, with a repeat showing likely only if the play were garlanded with awards. Now writers and directors could travel the world attending screenings of their new movies at festivals even before the venue for the London première had been negotiated. If successful, the films could have almost unlimited runs in the cinema before turning up on the shelves of video stores and eventually being screened on television. The acclaim given to films such as *My Beautiful Laundrette* and *Four Weddings and a Funeral* led to Hollywood offers for directors who had sometimes only been regarded as jobbing – although gifted – television practitioners. This chapter follows the rise of the low-budget British feature film and reveals how an enterprise that began as an attempt to extend the range and lifespan of the televison play turned into another phenomenon altogether: the calling card to Los Angeles.

Losing the Crown

During the early 1980s the BBC made yet another miscalculation about its drama department. Faced with the spiralling costs of making drama on film, it decided to reallocate resources among the various departments competing for funds. The Single Plays

department, one of the most prestigious within the BBC, would
have to face a cut in the number of films it could afford to produce. More *Plays for Today* would have to be made on tape in the
BBC's studios, thereby cutting costs and – it was hinted – artistic
self-indulgence at a stroke. Meanwhile valuable film resources
would be handed over to Jonathan Powell in the Series and Serials
department in order to compete with the increasing number of
ITV serials that were being shot on celluloid. Granada's award-
winning adaptations of *Brideshead Revisited* and *Hard Times* had
wounded the BBC's pride and it had become necessary to reassess
the way BBC classic serials were being made. Keith Williams, the
Head of Single Plays at the time, considered the decision to be a
sensible one.

With hindsight it was a catastrophic idea, at least for the future
of the single play at the BBC. Jonathan Powell's department proceeded to abandon classic serials in favour of contemporary ones.
From this remarkable period came *Edge of Darkness*, *The Singing
Detective* and *Tinker, Tailor, Soldier, Spy*. Each one of these had
the kind of narrative and lighting direction that one associates
with the cinema rather than television. Indeed, the directors of
both Kennedy Martin's *Edge of Darkness* and Potter's *The Singing
Detective* went on to make their careers in Hollywood, never to
return to British television. By the end of the 1980s, however, the
Single Plays department at the BBC had become something of a
damp squib. A respectable series of drama documentaries were
produced in the department, under Peter Goodchild, in the mid-
1980s, and of course Richard Eyre's *Tumbledown* ended the
decade with a spectacular impact. Today the department no longer
exits; ironically it is being absorbed into a subsidiary of the BBC's
current drama conglomerate known as BBC Films. Yet the real
mistake of the Single Plays department during the 1980s did not
only lie in handing over funds to Series and Serials. It also under-
estimated the influence of the newly arrived Channel 4 and its
unexpected declaration of support for the British film industry.

Channel 4 began broadcasting in November 1982. At the very
moment when the BBC began to abandon the single film, the fic-

tion department at Channel 4 gave the form its highest priority. This was due to the relationship between two remarkable men. Jeremy Isaacs, Channel 4's visionary and passionate first chief executive, appointed David Rose as his Head of Fiction. Rose, who had been running the BBC's regional drama department at Pebble Mill in Birmingham, arrived at Channel 4's Charlotte Street headquarters in London with a unique and instinctive understanding of the role of film in the history of television drama. As the original producer of the BBC's *Z Cars*, he had sat in the gallery at Television Centre while filmed inserts were played directly into the studio. Encouraged by Rose, the writers on *Z Cars* in the early 1960s – who included Troy Kennedy Martin, John McGrath and Alan Plater – had pioneered a fluid filmic style for the police series. A huge technical juggling act occurred weekly, as the series was transmitted live to viewers with a bold mix of studio and film. At Pebble Mill Rose had developed his interest in film in a manner that often went literally against the grain of the work being produced in London.

The BBC's basic attitude towards film was that you should shoot exterior scenes on celluloid and record interior scenes on tape in a multi-camera television studio. The former would provide around four minutes of cut material a day whereas the latter was expected to deliver over thirty minutes. Obviously film was the expensive option. In the early years filmed inserts into studio plays were shot on cumbersome 35mm cameras that were appropriate for feature films but not for the much tighter schedules of television drama. This changed in the early 1960s when producer Tony Garnett, going completely against the instructions of his superiors, went out to buy a 16mm camera in order to shoot *Cathy Come Home*. Garnett actually booked a television studio to record the interior scenes which was in fact only used for one token scene. *Cathy*, directed by Ken Loach, changed the face of television drama. Suddenly viewers were watching a story unfold in real locations, with the cutting and pace that they normally associated with the cinema. Inspired by the great Italian neo-realist directors and the French New Wave, Loach took the camera on to the streets, into

real council estates and pubs – mixing ordinary people in with his
actors. The realism of 1960s television drama was born. It is
important to note that, although Loach borrowed techniques from
the great film-makers of his day, he had no ambition to make a cinema film. Through an hour-long black and white *Wednesday Play*
Garnett and Loach could reach audiences of over 16 million.

It would be unfair to claim that the BBC produced no ambitious
drama on tape during the years following *Cathy*. The rule still
applied that film should only be employed on a script in which
exterior locations dominated. But gradually the best directors in
television came to be associated with celluloid rather than the elec-
tronic studio. Michael Apted, Mike Newell, Stephen Frears, John
Mackenzie, Mike Leigh, Roland Joffe all worked for the BBC and
ITV during these years, making memorable one-off films. At
BAFTA each year it was the film rather than the studio play that
won prizes and the applause of the profession. More importantly,
it often attracted the larger number of viewers. The neo-realist tradition of Loach was the dominant form for most of this period.
Yet, with the advent of colour television, BBC2 directors were able
to become more catholic in their choice of style. Stephen Frears
had begun his career with a low-budget feature film, *Gumshoe*, an
ironic homage to *The Maltese Falcon* brilliantly scripted by
Neville Smith. The films Frears made for the BBC and ITV during
the 1970s include gentle references to both Hollywood and
European cinema, as a counterpoint to the everyday stories being
told about Britain. As the directors became more confident and
skilled, so their ambitions for film grew. Philip Saville's *Gangsters*
commanded twice the normal *Play for Today* budget. Mike Leigh
needed an eight-week rehearsal period in order to shape a film like
Nuts in May with his actors.

David Hare's *Licking Hitler* (1978) symbolized a change in the
development of the television film. The script consisted almost
entirely of interior scenes set in a stately home during the Second
World War. BBC tradition dictated that the script would normally
be recorded in a television studio, but Hare persuaded David Rose
to make *Licking Hitler* as a film. Taking a chance on a first-time

director (as he was to do many times at Channel 4), Rose also let Hare take charge behind the camera. The result was a film that looked completely different from the normal BBC *Play for Today*. The majority of the films shot for television during this period did not really question the tradition of neo-realism. Often they looked and felt like a documentary, with the minimum use of artificial light and the emphasis on a moving camera tracking through real locations. Hare and his lighting cameraman, the late Ken Morgan, approached *Licking Hitler* in a completely different way. They turned the interior of a real stately home into a film studio. Each shot was lit according to the style of 1940s cinema. They high-lighted the contrast between light and shadow; the actor's face was often surrounded by darkness in order to convey an emotional effect. For the first time in a BBC film the camera did not move, apart from one long tracking shot towards the end. As in the still-ness of 1940s British cinema, a classical style powerfully domi-nated the action. The movement away from television and towards cinema had begun.

Rose wanted to build on this process at Channel 4. At a time when the BBC was questioning the cost and *raison d'être* of the single film, Rose committed a huge proportion of his budget to a slot that was to become known as *Film on 4*. The subsequent brain drain from the BBC was startling. Within a year of Channel 4's launch, Mike Leigh, David Hare, Stephen Frears, Richard Eyre and Philip Saville, among many others, had all abandoned the BBC for Charlotte Street. The directors knew Jeremy Isaacs was also a champion of film. At Thames Television he had been the executive producer of the marathon documentary series, *The World at War*. Spending hundreds of hours in the cutting room, often until the early hours of the morning, Isaacs came to love and respect the precision and painstaking search for truth that editing a film can sometimes constitute. In the company of directors like Frears and Hare he would talk passionately about European cin-ema, recalling his days spent queuing in a duffel coat outside the Everyman in Hampstead in order to see the latest Antonioni or Buñuel. Isaacs's arrival at Channel 4 coincided with a period he had spent as chairman of the British Film Institute's production board. There he became convinced that there was a role for the new television channel to play within the British film industry. He also became aware of film-makers like Peter Greenaway, Bill Douglas and Terence Davies, who had never found a home within the single-film tradition of the BBC.

At the time there was an absolute divide between the film and television industries. A film industry of sorts existed in the UK, but mainly to service the dying comic tradition of the *Carry On* farces or the latest James Bond extravaganza. Directors like Frears or Mike Leigh were firmly placed in the category of television directors with too small a vision for the big screen. On occasion the BBC had acknowledged the cinematic potential of some of its stock. But when a limited theatrical release was sought for *Gangsters*, the BBC's own unions refused to sign the agreement – effectively making it impossible for the BBC to show any of its films in a cinema. This is where the new channel was ahead of the game. Isaacs had decided that it would commission no in-house production. Everything would be bought in from independent producers who would be able to negotiate new agreements with the film unions. A team of commissioning editors was created to decide on the choice of productions. It is difficult to overstate how radical the decision was at the time. These days nearly everyone working in the upper or even lower echelons of television calls themselves a commissioning editor. At least one third of the workforce have left the BBC and ITV to become independent producers. But in 1982 very few people in television knew what an independent producer was or what a commissioning editor did.

The term commissioning editor comes from publishing rather than broadcasting. A commissioning editor at the new channel had first and foremost to apply editorial judgement to the hundreds of proposals that would land on his or her desk every week. In the case of the self-effacing David Rose, it was a doubly mysterious role to the outside world. For in order to get the backing of the industry to release his films in the cinema, it was agreed that the channel would adopt an extremely low profile. If you examine the early cinema posters for Neil Jordan's *Angel* (1982), Richard Eyre's *The Ploughman's Lunch* (1983) or Peter Greenaway's *The Draftsman's Contract* (1982), you will not find a credit for Channel 4. Yet the channel was often the major investor in the films, supplying up to between 50 and 90 per cent of their budgets. If you search very hard, you will find a credit for 'Film Four International', the name of the channel's sales company, though it is unlikely that many outside the distribution business would have recognized this title. Cinema distributors believed that the public would not pay to see a film in the cinema if they suspected it had been financed by a television company. So the nature of Channel 4's involvement in the success of these early films remained ambiguous.

The job of the independent producer was also a matter of some debate. Unlike their equivalents within the BBC or ITV, producers in the independent sector had complete financial control and responsibility over a film. A drama producer at the BBC would be responsible for the choice of script and director. He or she would be handed a budget, but had no way of knowing on a day-to-day basis whether or not the show might be over- or under-spending. The sums would only be added up on completion of the production. So working for Channel 4 meant learning new responsibilities and financial disciplines. It did not necessarily imply bringing extra money to the table. The channel was quite capable of fully funding a film to which it was committed. The choice of film was in fact based on an editorial, not a financial decision. Of the 300 *Films on 4* commissioned since 1982, only a tiny handful have seen a return on their initial investment. Isaacs and Rose regarded their brief as bringing to viewers the best new films rather than the most profitable. Several early commissions were for already existing screenplays that had not been able to find an outlet in the commercial market: Peter Greenaway's *The Draftsman's Contract* and Michael Radford's *Another Time, Another Place*, for example. Isaacs encouraged Rose to build links with European directors like Wim Wenders on *Paris Texas* (1984) and Andrei Tarkovsky on *The Sacrifice* (1986). Rose did not in fact accept a fundamental distinction between the best of film and television. His primary interest was in creating a strand for British film-makers that would have the widest possible constituency on television. Several of the early *Films on 4* had their first showings on television, not in the cinema. The opening night of Channel 4 saw the première of Stephen Frears's *Walter* which never gained a cinema release. Both *Angel* and *Another Time, Another Place* had very short runs in the cinema before being seen on television. Hollywood was very far from the thoughts of either Rose or Isaacs during the early years of *Film on 4*.

The profile of *Film on 4* changed during the mid-1980s with the commercial success of a number of its films. Ironically, the biggest success, *My Beautiful Laundrette* (1985), was never intended for cinema release at all. Rose had decided to commission part of his output purely for television. He would fully fund a handful of films that he felt would be unlikely to attract co-production money or the interest of a distributor. They would be shot on 16mm stock rather than the more expensive 35mm which was becoming increasingly common for *Film on 4*. In fact everyone working on the screenplay of *Laundrette*, including director Stephen Frears, had agreed they were making a controversial film for television rather than the cinema. 'It's like the old days,' Frears told me in pre-production. 'The kind of *Play for Today* we used to do at the Beeb. It's great. It'll cause a tremendous fuss.' Indeed a homosexual love affair between two young men – a National Front supporter and a Pakistani laundrette owner – set against the background of a drab and dismal South London might not seem the obvious candidate for worldwide renown. Yet *My Beautiful Laundrette* was the *Film on 4* that broke the mould. Screened at the Edinburgh Film Festival in the autumn of 1985, it had the film critics reaching for the kind of superlative about a contemporary British film they had not employed since the 1960s. The film won international success at the box office and an Oscar nomination for Hanif Kureishi's screenplay. Coupled with the success of Chris Bernard's *Letter to Brezhnev* in the same year, the perception grew that Channel 4 was now the prime mover and shaker in the British film industry.

From one point of view Channel 4 in the 1980s never quite recovered from this honeymoon period. After *Laundrette* only David Leland's *Wish You Were Here* (1987) achieved equivalent fame and popularity at the international box office. David Rose's taste and instinct was to encourage the kind of talent he had known at the BBC; whether or not this translated to box-office success in the cinema was a secondary consideration. He adored the way Michael Radford explored landscape as a primary shaper of drama in *Another Time, Another Place*. He had a relish for the method by which Mike Leigh created a film from the contribution of actors. Like Isaacs, he had an enthusiasm and gift for the small miracles that could transform a film in the cutting room. He was one of the few men to whom Peter Greenaway would listen after the screening of a rough cut. In Mike Figgis's performance art at the ICA he recognized the potential film-maker who would go on to make *Leaving Las Vegas*. To the first-time directors, like Figgis, Radford, Leland or Neil Jordan, he gave unlimited support even when it was accepted that their films might have difficulties with the distributors. He took over the tradition of the single film from the BBC, transformed it and left his rivals standing.

Making Movies

On Rose's departure from Charlotte Street in 1990, *Film on 4* was at something of a crossroads. Isaacs had also left the channel some three years earlier to run the Royal Opera House. Michael Grade had defected from his new job of managing director at the BBC in order to become Channel 4's second high-profile chief executive in a decade. Grade had a far more guarded approach to the relation- ship between television and cinema. At the BBC he discouraged his drama heads from trying to compete with Channel 4's feature-film output. He argued – quite correctly – that the licence payer had a right to see BBC drama premièred on television first rather than in the cinema or on video. Grade also felt that a flirtation with the cinema encouraged a streak of vanity in television producers and directors. Their sights would be set on attending glamorous world premières rather than on the needs of the viewer. So when Grade appointed David Aukin from the National Theatre as Rose's replacement, many felt that the writing was on the wall for *Film on 4*. Aukin came to the job with no experience of working in film or television and his own commitment as Head of Drama to *Film on 4* was unclear. Recent films had underperformed both on television and in the cinema. The signals he gave out to the profession were cautious and non-committal. Yet it soon became clear that a return to producing one-off films or plays purely for television was not a viable option. *Film on 4* had created an expectation among viewers and the profession that was unique in broadcasting, not just in this country but internationally. The revenue from co-production and box-office returns could never be equalled in television. Abandoning *Film on 4* would have meant giving up a huge amount of extra funding for the drama department at Channel 4. The clock, Aukin decided, could not be turned back. But the films had to turn into movies.

Aukin brought over a script assistant from Hollywood, Jack Lechner, to work on development. Swapping his National Theatre suit for a baseball cap and a collection of T-shirts, Aukin began to put his own stamp on *Film on 4*. After an admittedly shaky start – he had hardly been in a cutting room before Channel 4 – the results began to exceed all expectations. Peter Chesholm's *Hear My Song* was soon followed by Neil Jordan's Oscar-winning *The Crying Game* and Merchant-Ivory's *Howards End*. Then in 1994 came two other remarkable hits: Danny Boyle's *Shallow Grave* and of course Mike Newell's *Four Weddings and a Funeral*. Currently the standing of *Film on 4* remains high with the recent successes of *The Madness of King George* and *Trainspotting*. Neither has Aukin turned his back on the best talent that Rose nurtured. Ken Loach, Peter Greenaway and Mike Leigh continue to work for the slot, with the latter's remarkable *Naked* and *Secrets and Lies* winning the major prizes in Cannes in 1994 and 1996 (*Secrets and Lies* was also given an Oscar nomination for best direction in 1997).

It is significant that, while Rose spoke of commissioning films,

Aukin uses the word movie. In the midst of the current euphoria surrounding an apparently revived British film industry, including an injection of National Lottery money, it is worth considering what the shift from a television to a movie culture means for the writer. The current decline and standardization of so much television drama means that talented new writers will increasingly look to the cinema for their futures. Despite a so-called golden age of new writing now taking place in the theatre, most young playwrights are actually hard at work at their screenplays. The Bush Theatre has an informal relationship with the American film distributor Miramax to develop screenplays from successful stage productions. Jez Butterworth and Jonathan Harvey are merely two of the best young talents of the moment who first thought of both *Mojo* and *Beautiful Thing* as feature films rather than stage plays. The success of both plays in the theatre gave them the chance to write the screenplays. A decade ago they probably would not have had the opportunity; they would have been invited to write original pieces for television. Aukin has stated that one of the attractions of moving from the theatre to Channel 4 is that the majority of new plays in the theatre lack any narrative drive. Feature films have to tell a powerful story to succeed. Yet movies remain a director's medium, not a writer's. Paula Milne's four-part television serial for Channel 4, *The Politician's Wife*, will always be associated with her authorship. Yet her screenplay, *The Hollow Reed*, which the channel commissioned in the same year, became known as 'a film by Angela Pope' – that is, the director's. Nevertheless Aukin is aware of the danger of embracing Los Angeles too enthusiastically. British directors like Jon Amiel and Mick Jackson who have left for Hollywood now produce far worse work there than they once did for the BBC and Channel 4. Those who remain under the umbrella of British television – like Ken Loach and Mike Leigh – keep on getting better.

The most important *Film on 4* of the mid-1980s was *My Beautiful Laundrette* and that of the mid-1990s *Four Weddings and a Funeral*. *Laundrette*, shot masterfully on location by Stephen Frears, could have been a television *Play for Today*. It introduced the audience to a new writer's voice and a controversial theme, and it placed an unforgettable group of characters at the centre of drama. Mrs Whitehouse would have written to the BBC about it in a very vocal manner. *Four Weddings and a Funeral*, as Aukin has rightly claimed, is not a television film, in spite of the lack of special effects and violent action. The screenplay was in fact turned down by Nick Elliot at London Weekend and no BBC script editor at the time could have tolerated its seemingly uncritical celebration of an upper-middle-class lifestyle. The number of four-letter words that begin the film would probably not have been accepted by the BBC in what was supposed to be a light comedy. The broadcasters might also have had a problem with the lack of any real point to the film. It is true that there is no attempt to define any particular social truth in *Four Weddings*, unlike *Laundrette*. But it does in one sense touch something deeper about our times: the need to enter a world of pure celebration and indeed celebrities, to get as close to a movie as we can. The film was marketed in America and only opened in the UK as an already established hit. There is no question that, if it had premièred in Britain, it would not have had the same reviews or the same success. Those attending the London opening were already part of a hit. It is no coincidence that one of the people most closely associated with the movie, Elizabeth Hurley, was not actually in it. Somehow *Four Weddings* became a party for cinema to which the whole country was invited. The setting is a kind of modern-day Illyria, complete with its own *memento mori* at the end. But the real fun for the audience was in being part of a hit movie with a Hollywood star to wed in the final reel. It was a British dream that could only have its payoff by success in America. We all got our four minutes of fame out of it and who knows – as in Elizabeth Hurley's case – we might even be offered a contract in Los Angeles as a result.

Equally, Danny Boyle's *Shallow Grave* would never have seen the light of day on television. When Aukin showed the film to his fellow executives at Channel 4, we were horrified by its amorality. There seemed no dramatic justification for the violence. Yet a generation of film reviewers who had grown up with Tarantino and

Hollywood exploitation movies rallied to the cause. Whether the film will be remembered for the excellence of the screenplay rather than its undoubtedly effective directorial gore is still a matter for debate. In a less controversial arena, the smooth transition from stage to screen of Alan Bennett's *The Madness of King George* is again something television could not have contemplated in previous years. The co-financing of such projects is possible in the world of feature films as it would not be in television.

The BBC has reacted to the second wave of Channel 4's hits in a mood of depression and confusion. Although it has also commissioned several films in recent years that have been released theatrically – Anthony Minghella's *Truly, Madly, Deeply*, Stephen Frears's Roddy Doyle films and Jimmy McGovern's *Priest*, among others – a real profile in cinema has not been forthcoming. Perhaps this is not such a bad thing. Success at the box office should not become the sole criterion for writing screenplays in this country. Hollywood used to supply the world with a model of storytelling, in terms of dialogue, acting and direction. It still does on occasions. But now it is dominated by high-concept movies which are dependent on special effects and graphic violence in order to get audiences to buy tickets. The new movies often reveal an active contempt for dialogue and a complete lack of interest in human relationships. A talented British director like Jon Amiel, who gave BBC viewers *The Singing Detective*, is now responsible for Hollywood exploiters like *Copycat*. Mick Jackson, who delighted television viewers with *Threads*, *Life Story* and *A Very British Coup*, now sits by his West Coast swimming pool contemplating the fact that Kevin Costner had the last say in the final cut of *The Bodyguard*. There is such a thing as the devil's pact, at least in the entertainment industry.

It was Channel 4 that really enabled British writers to direct their own films for the first time. Under the old BBC and ITV system, the writer worked closely with the script editor and producer on several drafts of a script. The director would only become involved once a final draft had been agreed. This is in contrast to the feature-film industry, where a director and writer enter a long

period of development hell, spending months if not years together
before the finance for a production is finally agreed. But the new
television channel was often able to provide immediate backing
for films in which the director was clearly the team leader. Some
remarkable new directorial talent was discovered through the
process. Mike Figgis, Neil Jordan, Michael Radford, Peter
Greenaway, David Leland, Terence Davies and the late Bill
Douglas brought imagination to both the big and small screen.
Against all odds, our directors turned into the new auteurs of
Europe. None became more prominent than Mike Leigh.

Secrets and Lies – A Mike Leigh Film

In Mike Leigh's *Secrets and Lies* (1996) Timothy Spall plays a
photographer who is totally dedicated to his craft. In a series of
memorable collages we watch Spall's Maurice at work in his studio. There are sessions with brides and grooms to be, a nurse who
has spent fourteen years qualifying, an old woman with a cher-
ished Pekinese, lovers who are happy in each other's company and
husbands and wives who are clearly not. Spall approaches each of
his clients with understanding and the highest professional standards. He offers them all the opportunity to smile, though only a
small percentage accept. Many of the actors and actresses featured
in these cameo sequences are famous for their appearances in previous Mike Leigh films. Followers of his career will recognize,
among others, Liz Smith from *Hard Labour*, Sheila Kelley and
Antony O'Donnell from *Nuts in May*, Philip Davis and Ruth
Sheen from *High Hopes*, and of course Alison Steadman from
Abigail's Party and *Life Is Sweet*. The performers appear for mere
seconds on the screen but each one is able to tell us exactly what
we need to know about their characters – their private and public
selves, their secrets and lies – partly because of their acting talent
but also because of the way Spall (and by extension Leigh himself)
chooses to direct and photograph them.

   Secrets and Lies is a celebration of film-making – or, rather, of
the observational power that lies behind truly great cinema. It is

no coincidence that two of the main characters in the film are involved in ocular activities. Spall is the professional photographer dedicated to bringing a measure of truth and understanding to the chaos of his family's manifold self-deceptions, while Hortense, the black optician played by Marianne Jean-Baptiste, sets out on a journey of real discovery when the mother who adopted her dies. But the film is also a vindication of Leigh's own career as one of the great observers of recent years. Every frame, every movement of the camera or change of angle becomes a triumphant insight into a character's secret motivation or feeling. *Secrets and Lies* is above all a film about faces – one of the most powerful since Bergman's *Persona* – where real pain lies behind a smile and language is often a barrier to the truth.

Strictly speaking, of course, Leigh is not a writer at all. His scripts are devised with his actors over a long and demanding period of rehearsal. Since his first feature, *Bleak Moments* (1971), Leigh has always demanded a huge act of faith on the part of his patrons. Not a word of a script exists before the commencement of pre-production. There is still a great deal of ambiguity surrounding how much he actually knows about a script on the first day of rehearsal. His work has frequently been criticized for letting an individual performer run away with a show in a grotesque and sometimes heartless manner. Although the BBC tolerated Leigh for a while, there is no question that it was the advent of *Film on 4* that provided him with a continuity of work that has led to a masterpiece like *Secrets and Lies*. The five major films he has made for the channel since *Meantime* in 1983, following six television films at the BBC in the 1970s, have been an object lesson in sheer dogged persistence. It is sometimes said that Leigh has been lucky to find patronage for his demanding method of work. The same eyebrows are raised at the National Theatre's support of David Hare or at the BBC and Channel 4's backing of Bleasdale and Potter. Max Stafford-Clark has claimed that the majority of writers have short careers and tend to burn out in their mid-thirties. Yet Leigh, Hare, Bleasdale and Potter have reaped the rewards of simply sticking at things. The majority of writers are not as ambitious – not simply

for themselves but for the actual scale of the work. Few, like Hare,
are actually prepared to write for the massive space of the Olivier
stage as opposed to the Cottesloe. The majority of directors are
not willing – like Leigh – to embark on a major film without a single line of dialogue in place. Although it has become fashionable to
think the opposite it is harder to write an episode of *GBH* than of
Soldier Soldier.

Leigh's films are always distinguished by extraordinary work
from the actors. In *Secrets and Lies* no single performer steals the
show, but Brenda Blethyn as the photographer's sister is an unforgettable presence. Cynthia is an accident waiting to happen. She
lives in the rundown house of her parents, attempting to supervise
the upbringing of her illegitimate teenage daughter. The flicker of
her eyelids, the pain and puzzlement in her eyes, constantly stress
her best intentions – which surface as the commonest of Cockney
platitudes. 'You all right, swede-heart?' she asks her daughter, who
clearly isn't. 'Chance would be a fine thing,' she pronounces when
it is suggested she might be going out with a man. When she learns
from Hortense, the black optician, that she may be her mother, she
bursts into tears. 'No offence, swede-heart,' she tells the girl. 'I'd
have remembered, wouldn't I?' It is clear at this point that she
doesn't remember sleeping with a black man and is only embarrassed for Hortense. Seconds later the truth dawns on her. Tear-
stained and ghostlike, her face tells us that she indeed remembers
Hortense's father. 'Oh . . . bloody hell,' is her line, but the tears are
for herself this time. Mike Leigh holds the long encounter between
the two women in a Holborn café on a two-shot as we watch their
reactions to every nuance of the conversation simultaneously. It is
a beautiful moment of cinema which in more conventional hands
would have undoubtedly been directed as two separate close-ups.
The direction of Blethyn's performance is totally confident. The
camera often keeps its distance, encircling her before coming in for
a more painful close-up. When her brother visits her for the first
time in two years, he is appalled that she has held on to so much of
their parents' junk. In a wide shot Cynthia visibly collapses. 'Give
me a cuddle, Maurice . . . please, swede-heart.' As she moves into

her brother's arms, Leigh holds the shot and photographs the scene with Cynthia's back to us. Certainly the majority of television directors would have cut to a reverse close-up of her in tears. Yet Leigh's choice is the more moving.

The film is far more than simple observation of character. The story of Hortense searching for her real mother has genuine mystery and suspense. The fact that a young black girl discovers her real mother to be white produces a narrative of real charm and originality. Even when we learn that Cynthia is her mother, we wonder how the racial theme will be resolved. Part of Leigh's achievement is to treat the story in purely human terms. Hortense and Cynthia clearly adore each other and are able to share a mother–daughter relationship that neither has experienced before. But Leigh's metaphor of a working-class family coming to terms with black Britain is a new one. It is curious how our directors – with the notable exception of Stephen Frears in *Black Christmas* and *My Beautiful Laundrette* – have tended to ignore the subject. A director as socially aware as Ken Loach, for instance, has never tackled racism. One suspects that left-wing directors in Britain may have avoided the issue because it rarely makes heroes out of the working class. For Leigh to have introduced the subject in such a touching yet significant way is an undoubted breakthrough.

Yet he does so without the baggage of an issue-based drama. The style and pace of the film would in fact have been instantly recognizable to the great practitioners of European cinema. The birthday-party sequence in which Maurice produces hamburgers, steaks and sausages for his family is contained in a single wide shot. An entire family comes to life before us – dispassionate, neurotic and comic – almost as a play within a play. Hollywood does not tolerate such experiments with the camera. Mike Leigh will never be part of the flight to California. When British directors succeed in America it is, as Michael Apted said of *The Coalminer's Daughter*, because they have treated their work exactly as a *Play for Today*. The films the Americans most respect from British directors, whether by Leigh, Neil Jordan or Stephen Frears, are the ones they could not make themselves. It is by giving support to directors who are in opposition to Los Angeles that *Film on 4* has won its greatest accolades.

Auteurs Anonymous

The move towards a cinema-based culture, however, has been a mixed blessing for writers who, unlike Mike Leigh, do not direct – and even sometimes for those who do. After *Licking Hitler* David Hare never quite delivered a film with the same attack and polish, though he went on to write and direct three theatrical features for Channel 4. Stephen Poliakoff's direction of his own work has not yet catapulted one of his films into the premier league. The jury is still out on whether a gifted writer like Christopher Hampton shows an equal flair as a director. It is also true, however, that the vast majority of directors in this country are not writers and often have a fairly narrow vision of what a movie should be. Many of them, particularly the younger generation, will have been influenced by one of the expensive weekend courses that the American Robert McKee gave in London during the late 1980s. At these extraordinary events the bombastic professor would claim to reveal the secret formula behind each and every successful Hollywood movie in front of a hushed and reverent group of film students, BBC script editors and freelance directors. The carrot being dangled in front of people at such occasions was success in Hollywood. That is why directors will often tell writers to simplify dialogue, increase the number of action sequences and leave some space for improvisation with the actors. For they see their movie – be it shot for Channel 4, the BBC or British Screen – as a 'calling card' to the city where their craft can then be taken truly seriously. In a paradoxical way the increased power of directors is leading to the absence of the writer from the set and the film-making process in general.

Meanwhile the European cinema has fallen upon its own sword. When Leigh, Frears, Apted, Loach and Newell were working in British television, Antonioni, Fellini, Buñuel, Truffaut, Malle and Bergman were still active as continental film-makers.

That culture is now part of another time and place. There are no directors working in European cinema in the mid-1990s to compare with the great names of the 1950s and 1960s. Yet the cult of the auteur – the writer taking on the direction of his or her own script – continues unabated. Directors counter this argument by claiming that most scripts written in this country are too rooted in a literary culture and lack real visual excitement. They need opening out and invariably less dialogue. But this is to misunderstand a great deal about the movies. From the 1930s to the 1950s, Hollywood was completely part of a literary tradition in which the writers and producers shaped the script, not the director. The films were entirely dependent on dialogue and economic storytelling. The director's contribution was of course crucial; but no stars would have been made without great lines and no cinemas would have been packed without wonderful stories to screen. Certainly, the belief in the director as auteur begins with the French New Wave – partly, of course, because Godard and Truffaut wanted to write and direct their own films. Yet in spite of their championing of cult Hollywood directors over producers and screenwriters, Godard and in particular Truffaut remain considerable literary figures. Truffaut's correspondence is not packed with as many comments on his favourite films as one might expect. But practically every letter refers to his reading and love of books. In *Fahrenheit 451* the true nightmare of the future is not a world without movies but a world without novels. It is the burning of the books by the Nazis which finally persuades Jules and Jim that their civilized bohemian lives are coming to a close.

Truffaut's own films make constant reference to his reading: diaries are read out, poems are quoted in voiceover, his characters actually enter bookshops to buy the latest paperbacks. This is more than a matter of literacy. Reading the great novels of the past gave Truffaut a knowledge of storytelling that no present-day course on film direction provides. His work as a film-maker benefited from his reading. The broad range of his understanding and of literary tradition bring a charm and strength to his stories that has now almost disappeared from French cinema. It was equally

true of Louis Malle's work – and of all the great humanist directors who emerged in Europe both before and after the Second
World War. Renoir, Rossellini, Buñuel and Fellini had an appetite
for life and a knowledge of the human heart that enriched the cinema but did not exclusively derive from it. They are the real
auteurs, whose ambitions took them a long way from directing car
chases or shoot-outs on an LA freeway.

5 The Critics

I miss our duelling days. The trouble with our successors is that
nothing seems *at stake* for them.

— Kenneth Tynan in a letter to Harold Hobson

Intellectual disgrace
Stares from every human face

— W. H. Auden, 'In Memory of W. B. Yeats'

The late Robert Stephens had the most honest take on critics. He
would cite the case of a fellow actor on reading an unfavourable
review of his performance by Harold Hobson in the *Sunday Times*.
'That bastard Hobson!' Stephens's colleague would rant over the
coffee and marmalade. 'Done it again. Completely cocked up.' The
actor would then begin a long diatribe against Hobson and everything the man stood for, consigning him finally to that particularly
unpleasant circle in Dante's hell that is, at least in an actor's imagination, reserved for ungrateful theatre critics. A few months later
the same actor would be at the breakfast table reading another
review by Hobson – this time favourable – of his most recent performance. 'Good old Harold,' he'd smile contentedly. 'You can
always rely on him to get it right.'

Theatre

No one who works in theatre, film or television can possibly fail to
recognize the syndrome. A critic whom one may have previously
denounced as crass and incompetent is suddenly elevated to the status of near genius simply because he or she has chosen to give you a
good review. Criticism is a notoriously subjective business and readers of newspapers probably pay less attention to good or bad
notices than practitioners often imagine. Nevertheless, the cultural
climate in which new plays, television serials or films are received
does matter. When Kenneth Tynan was reviewing for the *Observer*

during the early 1960s, with Harold Hobson as his opposite number on the *Sunday Times*, there was genuine excitement and debate
surrounding every first night of a new play at the Royal Court or
Royal Shakespeare Company. When overnight reviews for a risk-
taking new play were lukewarm, the theatres would hold their
breath and wait for the Sunday notices. Invariably, Hobson and
Tynan would have something decisive and surprising to say. They
would often quarrel with each other in public, disagreeing about
their actual reasons for liking a play, but nevertheless in tandem
they created a huge appetite in the reader to go and see it.

As a sixth-former at a London grammar school in the early
1960s, I can vouch for the fact that our whole class would be discussing Tynan and Hobson on a Monday morning. Tynan was the
more favoured, of course; he had taken up the cause of Brecht and
socialism, deliberately appealing to a new meritocracy among the
Observer's readership that would elevate John Osborne's Jimmy
Porter to a commanding position in British society as well as theatre. Hobson was a far more conservative and godfearing man.
His attraction was to the Middle England of his day: readers of the
Sunday Times who enjoyed the plays of Coward and Rattigan but
who now, Hobson insisted, had also to come to terms with Beckett
and Ionesco. He would usually tell his readers in complete sincerity how religious the plays were. Penelope Gilliat, the *Observer*'s
film critic at the time, once wrote that the characteristic sound of
an English Sunday morning was that of Harold Hobson 'barking
up the wrong tree'. Yet in hindsight he brought an enquiring conservative audience to the new drama – with money to spend at the
box office – that Tynan might never have reached with his more
fashionable appeal to the young.

I doubt whether students in today's sixth-form colleges are discussing theatre reviews on Monday mornings. One reason may be
that there are almost no theatre critics under thirty writing regu-
larly for any of the broadsheets. It was noticeable that nearly every
critic reviewing Richard Eyre's production of Ibsen's *John Gabriel
Borkman* (1996, National Theatre) related Paul Scofield's performance in the central role to his *King Lear*. There was an assump-

tion that readers of the notices would have seen Scofield playing Lear. Yet Peter Brook's production of the play happened almost thirty-five years ago. (The film version bears almost no relation to the original.) No reader under the age of fifty would have stood a chance of actually having seen Scofield in the role. It is therefore unsurprising that sixth-formers or students today do not cancel engagements on a Saturday night to queue for returns at the Royal Court because of a review in the *Observer* or the *Sunday Times*. Their idea of criticism is in any case more likely to come from *Time Out*, where a paragraph is considered adequate space to print a notice in which to recommend or condemn a play. When there is a fuss, as with the outcry over Sarah Kane's *Blasted* at the Theatre Upstairs, the debate is almost entirely confined to the newspapers and rarely spreads to an argument among the audience, as was the case with Edward Bond's *Saved*. Theatre critics today have plenty of opinions. They champion new writers and directors. They conscientiously travel the country in search of fresh talent. Yet they never seem to disagree with each other in a manner that finally interests the public.

For the best new plays cause disagreement, not agreement. Peter Hall tells the story that, after the first night of *Waiting for Godot* at the Arts Theatre in 1955, half the audience cheered and the other half booed. That is the sign of a healthy new play. New talent divides rather than unites the critics. The newspapers did attempt to raise a debate about *The Absence of War* at the National, yet in this instance editors had to enlist the support of journalists and politicians rather than reviewers to achieve their ends. The only way to get the story on the news pages was to have known politicians and high-profile parliamentary reporters writing about it. The regular reviewers had their own say, but as a kind of critical damp squib in less accessible areas of the papers. It is impossible to believe that either Tynan or Hobson would have tolerated this situation. But their typewriters might have found the words to rise above mere reportage whereas the laptops and modems of their present-day successors rarely do. Yet the majority of practising theatre critics today do see themselves – wrongly, in

my view – as the legitimate heirs of Tynan and Hobson. Most of
them have been around for a very long time. The two Michaels –
Billington and Coveney – began writing for the *Guardian* and the
Financial Times respectively more than twenty years ago. Nicholas
de Jongh of the *Evening Standard* began his career as a critic more
than thirty years ago as Billington's second stringer on the
Guardian. Irving Wardle, who was actually Kenneth Tynan's
deputy at the *Observer* in 1959, only recently retired from his post
of theatre critic on the *Independent on Sunday*. Some years ago his
more prestigious role as daily theatre critic of *The Times* became
the responsibility of Benedict Nightingale, whose critical music
was first heard in the pages of *Plays & Players* and the *New
Statesman* in the mid-1960s.

Michael Billington and Benedict Nightingale have both gone on
record to argue that British theatre is currently going through a
golden age of new writing. 'I cannot recall,' stated Billington in a
Guardian article dated 13 March 1996, 'a time when there were
so many exciting dramatists in the twentysomething age-group:
what is more they seem to be speaking to audiences of their own
generation.' He cites new plays by Jez Butterworth, Sarah Kane
and David Eldridge, among others. Benedict Nightingale's list of
new playwrights in a *Times* article dated 1 May 1996 includes
Kane and Butterworth, but goes on to praise works by others such
as Simon Bent, Joe Penhall and Judy Upton. Nightingale's article
begins with a reference to Tom Stoppard: 'Tom Stoppard once said
he became a playwright because John Osborne's *Look Back in
Anger* caused such a stir that the theatre was clearly "the place to
be at". There is a similar buzz in the air now . . .'

Except there isn't. No one would wish to detract from the
promise of Butterworth's *Mojo*, Sarah Kane's *Blasted* or Nick
Grosso's *Peaches*, but these works are not known to the public in
the way that John Osborne's *Look Back in Anger* or Arnold
Wesker's *Roots* were in the 1950s, largely due to their championing by Tynan and Hobson. There is no real debate about these
new plays or their subject matter. They do not seem to suggest the
kind of metaphor that might get an audience talking about their

content and meaning. There is a vague feeling on the part of Billington and Nightingale that young people are becoming interested in theatre again – and that they are bringing their love of Tarantino and *Coronation Street* to the occasion. They suggest that the new young writers should command our interest without explaining why. Nightingale is almost apologetic about his enthusiasm: 'All have had premières at the Royal Court and its Theatre Upstairs or at the Bush Theatre . . . unlike the dramatists that preceded them, these writers have no obvious political credo, no social agenda, and take a quizzical view of human nature.'

In other words, unlike Osborne, Pinter, Shaffer, Brenton or Hare, these new writers – at least according to Nightingale – have almost nothing to say. Neither Billington nor Nightingale can come up with a reason for going to see these plays other than the fact that they are written by the young and have 'a quizzical view of human nature'. If that had been the platform for championing Osborne or Beckett during the 1950s, absolutely no one would have turned up at the box office. Jimmy Porter, Vladimir and Estragon were far more important dramatic characters of their day than that. But Billington and Nightingale make almost no reference to the actual content of the new plays: a new way of storytelling that might attract us, performances which will move or excite. They feel they don't have to do this except on a minimal level, and so the real work of a critic is left out of the equation. They assume readers will support a culture of new writing purely for its own sake. But this has never been the reality in theatre, film or television. As the profile of new writing declines, as the number of opportunities fall, so the call to support new writing intensifies.

During the past few years BBC2 has practically killed off viewers' appetite for new writing by presenting an interminably dreary series of single films under the *Screen Two* label. Week after week we were presented with the bleakest portraits of life in Britain that have probably ever been conceived, which were then written and directed in the most depressing way imaginable. As a tale of incest in the inner city followed a bloody account of drug-taking in the inner city, so the BBC announcer would prepare us for the subject matter of next week's film: a harrowing account of homelessness in the inner city. Many of the films were praised by the television critics and picked up awards around the world. Spending on average around £800,000 per film, the BBC started to panic when audience figures fell below a million. Obviously the business needs to attract new talent; it will not survive without the young coming into it. But to make a fetish of new writing when the plays themselves have little appeal to audiences is a self-defeating exercise. Audiences will not pay for a seat at the theatre or turn on a television play because it is a worthy thing to do. This is not to attack the young or the work currently being produced at the Bush Theatre or the Royal Court's Theatre Upstairs. But it is critical tomfoolery to suggest that a new *Look Back in Anger* is being discovered each month. In fact there is no evidence that every generation produces dramatists of real distinction. Greek tragedy and comedy flourished for about seventy years, the Elizabethan and Jacobean theatre for an even shorter span of time. There is little reason to believe that the movement begun by George Devine and Tony Richardson in 1956 will necessarily last for ever.

In any case Billington and company have been round this particular mulberry bush before. During the 1980s, as public interest in new writing began to wane, theatre critics began overpraising rather than underpraising plays. Osborne and Pinter were given a rather rocky ride by reviewers throughout their careers. Yet the work of Louise Page, Sarah Daniels and Kevin Hood, produced at the Royal Court during Max Stafford-Clark's regime, was given a rather easy critical ride in comparison. All three of these dramatists currently earn their living by writing popular serials on radio and television, which is not the outcome that many reviewers predicted for their talents. At the same time the critics often failed to notice that the true inheritors of the George Devine tradition at the Court were not in fact the British but the new American writers. In this instance our critics' nationalism did not serve them well. For it is the plays of David Mamet, Tony Kushner and Wallace Shawn that stand the test of a decade. One can see a similar tendency among film critics today to overpraise British films. The majority want to believe in the culture of a new-born film industry and so will often give unmerited space to a film simply because it has been shot and financed in this country. Critics may have the best intentions in creating the myth of a golden age of new writing in the theatre or of British talent dominating Hollywood, yet the final result of this intellectual dishonesty is to make us question their own power and judgement.

Indeed that is what their own editors are increasingly doing. Reviewing plays is not the fashionable trade it used to be. Theatre critics in particular have failed to read the new writing on the wall. Arts editors are looking to cut back on individual review space to make way for the larger think piece or what 'The Culture' section of the *Sunday Times* once referred to as 'The Essay'. The truth is that the assumptions behind theatre and film reviewing are rather despised by the new generation of arts editors. They want the buzz that comes from an individual column: new voices that treat the arts world with the lack of seriousness they feel it deserves. When 'The Culture' first began, it downgraded reviewing – with the exception of television – to the humble status of the *Time Out* caption review. 'The Culture' invariably devotes most of the space reserved for film criticism to the most hyped movie of the week rather than the best: Pamela Anderson Lee in *Barbed Wire* will always take precedence over anything more complex. The new columnists actively despise the notion that writers are important, particularly in film or television. In the spring of 1996 A. A. Gill took time out from his cookery and television columns in the *Sunday Times* to write a long article on Dennis Potter. The piece coincided with the launch of Potter's last works, *Karaoke* and *Cold Lazarus*, on the BBC and Channel 4. Gill did not of course review the two serials. That would have distracted him from his true end, which was to point out that individual writers had nothing left to contribute to British television drama. The era of Potter, Bleasdale, Lynda La Plante and Jack Rosenthal was now thankfully over, he declared. 'Most American television is a Normandy Landing; most British television is Dunkirk,' wrote Gill. 'The future and nature of

television is in co-operative, multi-authored pieces.' In other
words, just hand over the keys of British television to Rupert
Murdoch and let him get on with the job.

This view is not confined to the *Sunday Times* or even to newspapers. The last ten years have seen most arts programming on
television making the same point. *The Late Show* on BBC2, for
instance, was very rarely concerned with describing or analysing
individual writing talent. It had a much sharper identity than that
in its relish for the culture of the put-down. Producers on the show
didn't call it that, of course. They used phrases like the decon-
struction of talent or the demystification of the authorial voice.
But putting down talent became *The Late Show*'s favourite sport.
Each week a panel of three guests, chaired first by Sarah Dunant,
then by Mark Lawson, would lay into a play, film or television
drama like three dogs at a bone. For they wouldn't let go until at
least one of the panel – preferably all three – had taken a show and
torn it to pieces. The programme was considered to be a failure if
all three panellists had actually liked something. I will never forget
a discussion about Peter Hall's 1995 production of *Hamlet* which
celebrated the opening of the newly titled Gielgud Theatre in the
West End. Two of the panel – Alison Pearson from the
Independent on Sunday and most recently the *Observer* and Tony
Parsons of the *Daily Telegraph* – admitted to disliking the play
almost more than the production. The third – Ulsterman Tom
Paulin – growled his disapproval at the fact that the director had
obviously not read Jan Kott's *Shakespeare Our Contemporary* and
given the production the kind of modern slant that Shakespeare
cried out for. Paulin was not to know that some thirty years earlier
Hall had first introduced Stratford-upon-Avon and London audiences to Kott's book and indeed had used it for the basis of an
influential production of *Hamlet* starring David Warner in 1965.

But Alison Pearson's comments were the most revealing. She
had been amused to notice a sixth-form girl in the audience
mouthing the words of the text to herself as the actors spoke the
same lines on stage. The girl seemed to be deeply moved. Pearson
ridiculed the spectacle and attacked the production for cynically

appealing to the A-level crowd. The idea that someone might actually like a play, be moved to learn it by heart and become further
entranced by a performance of it in a theatre is not a concept that
The Late Show ever took seriously. In Wallace Shawn's latest play,
The Designated Mourner (1996), we are introduced to a semi-
futuristic society in which those who love culture are destroyed by
those who hate it. A woman's love of theatre is suddenly eroded
when she is told by an acquaintance that a performance she particularly admired was trite and the acting much too broad. Readers
of A. A. Gill's article on Dennis Potter in the *Sunday Times* will not
have sat down to watch the opening episode of *Karaoke* that same
day with an open mind. In *The Designated Mourner* Mike Nichols
played a character who admits that he has learnt to love the fact
that he is lowbrow. That was finally the effect of *The Late Show*: it
was jealous of real talent and individual creativity. In this it was
similar to the *J'Accuse* strand in Channel 4's *Without Walls*, which
in its last days masqueraded as an arts programme by having Tony
Parsons talk to us about the foreskin and Janet Street-Porter
attacking the Internet. These shows turned us all into lowbrows.

Television

In this process no one was more instrumental than the television
critic Clive James. Before James arrived on the reviewing scene in
the 1970s television criticism – at least in the broadsheets – tended
to concentrate on the more serious programmes. James altered the
balance through a series of influential and often hilarious columns
in the *Observer* that tended to place *Dallas* at the top of his
reviewing priorities rather than *Play for Today*. He started to enjoy
parodying the mannerisms of the sports commentators and their
comparative lack of skill with the English language. James also
adored the schlock serials and devoted more column inches to *The
Brothers* than he ever did to single plays or documentaries. Unlike
many of his successors, James did not write out of envy or mali-
ciousness. He did not want the small screen to be entirely free from
the presence of serious artists; he just didn't find them as much fun

to write about as Virginia Wade at Wimbledon or Cliff Richard on *Top of the Pops* (how he would have relished their improvised 1996 double-act at Wimbledon during the rain!). James was half in love with the television personalities he ridiculed so effectively in his column each week and he left journalism to become one himself. Today he hosts a series of middlebrow chat-shows on television, forever beaming at us with twinkling eyes and seemingly content in his move from critic to performer.

James's effect on television criticism was considerable, however. Each of his successors tries to emulate his style. The broadsheet review columns are now packed with pieces about the soaps, the mishaps of commentators and the hairpieces of morning chat-show presenters. The message is clear: television has become a totally trivial medium. Each Sunday A. A. Gill apes a critical style that is part fogey, part fool and 100 per cent philistine. Auschwitz, he tells us, is far too difficult a subject for a popular medium like television to handle. Sometimes you have to search quite hard in the other Sunday papers – especially the broadsheets – for any clear views about the new documentaries or drama. The plethora of cop shows and hospital dramas have been manna from heaven for the post-Jamesian reviewers. Each week they can have as much fun as they like without having to come up with anything that resembles a serious opinion about a writer. This is not to argue against humour in television criticism. Nancy Banks-Smith of the *Guardian*, for instance, is often mistakenly placed in the same camp as Clive James. In fact her brilliant comic prose is based on a love and respect for the medium, not on a feeling of superiority.

It has been a long time since a reviewer in theatre, film or television has written about, let alone championed, the work of a particular writer over more than one piece of work. Yet Tynan and Hobson would not be remembered today if they had merely written wittily about the theatre of their time. They followed the careers of the writers they admired consistently and passionately, and they frequently told them what they were doing wrong. In their columns they were not afraid to discuss the ideas and themes behind a play. As far as television drama is concerned, there used to be very little written about it at all. Television playwrights would look with envy at the kind of coverage their opposite numbers in the theatre could command. This too has changed. Whereas single plays on television still struggle for attention from the papers, the amount of space devoted to television series and serials can be overwhelming. It is the nature of the coverage that is different. Television critics now divide themselves into two camps: the previewers and reviewers. They will frequently disagree about a programme in the same newspaper, yet no debate or exchange of views between previewer and reviewer will ever appear in print. Both will often have been primed on the background of a new series by other feature articles in the newspaper. The emphasis in these pieces will have been on the overall budget of a show, its expected performance in the ratings battle between ITV and the BBC and its importance to the profile of the channel that commissioned it. There will be very little discussion about the drama itself.

The première of Potter's two last serials is a case in point. Almost every newspaper carried major articles about the event. At first the coverage was extremely respectful, reporting the way in which the BBC and Channel 4 had combined forces to fulfil Potter's dying request. It is true that the £10 million budget also got a fair share of the headlines. But about three weeks before transmission the emphasis changed. In early April 1996 the BBC held a launch for its forthcoming season in which extracts from both *Karaoke* and *Cold Lazarus* were shown. It was obvious to the assembled hacks that the shows contained more F-words than were common on BBC1 on a Sunday night. Articles appeared both condemning and attacking the serials. Reviewers got hold of bootleg copies and began to rush into print to deliver the first verdict on the final Potters. Mark Lawson in the *Guardian* reviewed the programmes without having seen them. A hasty reading of the scripts was enough to persuade him that the careers of all great writers take a downward spiral towards the end of their lives. Yet it was Lawson who got the plots of both serials wrong. The *Evening Standard* told its readers to stand by for a heady mix of foul language and graphic sex, even though the editor knew that the show contained very little material of this kind. It was as though the whole emphasis lay upon a man's reputation rather than his work. It was Potter the icon of British television that mattered, not the plays themselves. The interest was in the way Potter was seen as 'blackmailing' powerful television executives into giving in to his dying wishes on the back of the licence payer. I doubt whether many of the journalists who wrote about *Karaoke* and *Cold Lazarus* so heatedly before transmission ever bothered to watch them actually go out on television. They were not interested in reviewing the drama, only the reputation of the writer. In fact, when the serials were premièred at the National Film Theatre a week before transmission, only one member of the press bothered to attend.

The idea that a new work can divide as well as unite audiences and critics would not have been unfamiliar to Tynan or Hobson. A good play meant that there could also be a serious argument about it. Yet somehow the myth has grown up that present-day reviewers need to be unanimous in their praise before a show can be judged a hit. This is a sure way for mediocre and uncontroversial drama to rise to the top. Throughout his career Potter always divided the critics. *The Singing Detective* appalled as many of its early review-ers as it delighted others. Yet people today resent a difference of opinion and even refuse to acknowledge it. Looking at the reviews of *Karaoke*, it is true that A. A. Gill called it 'simply dreadful – flabby dialogue, pointlessly unattractive characters and a plot that is complex and convoluted without the promise of interest'. Peter Paterson in the *Daily Mail* told his readers that it was a brilliant swansong, 'a bringing together of all the strands that made Potter pre-eminent among writers for TV'. In the *Evening Standard* A. N. Wilson described the opening episode of *Karaoke* as 'the last word in drivel'. The same edition of the newspaper carried a rave review by Victor Lewis-Smith, calling it a great piece of writing and direc-tion. Yet it would be impossible to put these four very different reviewers on a platform and engage them in any kind of debate about Potter's last works. The four men would have nothing to say to each other. The game is up once an opinion-maker has to acknowledge the existence of another of his or her tribe. The last thing they can afford to admit is that other opinions might matter more than their own. All opinions must be seen as equally valid; and therefore no one view can ever be allowed to become authoritative. However, one thing does remain clear about newspaper coverage of television drama in this country. Mud sticks.

Film

Film critics have a far more distinguished track record in this country than their colleagues on the television pages. From the 1930s onwards, some of our best writers have chosen to test their critical prose out on the new art form of the twentieth century. Among others, Graham Greene was a formidable film critic during the 1930s – his hard-edged love of cinema leading to a new career as a screenwriter by the end of the decade. After the Second World War a host of distinguished names led intelligent opinion about the cinema on the arts pages of the *Observer* and the *Sunday Times*. C. A. Lejeune, Dilys Powell, Penelope Gilliat and George Melly covered the canvas of film in a manner that was entertaining but entirely responsible. Good criticism was not confined to the broadsheets. Many of the tabloids began to carry film reviews that were both highly informed and extremely challenging for their readers. In the 1960s the new wave of British cinema that led to *Saturday Night and Sunday Morning*, *A Taste of Honey* and *The Servant* was supported equally by the lowbrow and highbrow press. After more than twenty-five years at the *Evening Standard*, Alexander Walker still has one of the most polished and provocative prose styles of any critic in the country.

Part of the interest of being a film critic is that one is only occasionally reviewing the work of British talent. Film critics today may have become a touch over-indulgent about covering new British cinema, but at best British films only account for a tiny proportion of the output of world cinema. From the beginning British critics were reviewing an essentially American art form. Their style would often be laconic and satirical. No British critic would ever take *Gone with the Wind* quite as seriously as their American counterparts. It was a very long time before a British critic ever wrote well about a Hollywood musical. But nevertheless they opened a critical gateway to a new form of mass entertainment. Essentially, it was their job to welcome it. It is interesting that women have played a role in film criticism that they have never quite managed in either television or theatre. Storytelling in the cinema is closer to novel-writing than either theatre or television, with the possible exception of the television serial. Dilys Powell, Penelope Gilliat and Pauline Kael have brought a nuance to their critical writing that has often eluded the men. Both Jane Austen and George Eliot would have been very fine film critics. One does not feel quite as sure about Dickens or Hardy.

Paradoxically, however, the real strength of film criticism in this country lay in its love of the Continent. After the war the great European directors were consistently championed by English critics. Gilliat, Melly and Powell encouraged a generation of readers to queue up outside the Academy in Oxford Street, the Everyman at Hampstead or the Curzon in Piccadilly to watch an epoch-making cycle of subtitled films from Sweden, Italy, France and Eastern Europe. C. A. Lejeune in the *Observer* began this tradition with her enthusiasm for the films of Jean Renoir. Here was a poet of cinema, she told *Observer* readers, whose eye matched that of a great painter and whose ear the finest dialogue of a master novelist. The films of Bergman, Antonioni, Fellini and Buñuel met with a similar response.

Although a schoolboy at the time, I can still remember reading Penelope Gilliat's staunch defence of Antonioni's controversial *La Notte* (1961) in the *Observer*. There is a sequence in which Jeanne Moreau abandons her husband – played by Marcello Mastroianni – and takes a long walk through the streets of Milan. The camera simply observes her and the environment for some ten minutes. Gilliat insisted that the episode revealed more than just the end of a relationship. Behind Moreau's eyes was a vacuum, but her body movement was highly charged. Workers in the street turned to look at her with awe and wonder. Faced with the stalemate of

1960s Europe – its anonymous tower blocks and spiritual bore-dom – a woman had only one asset to command. Moreau walks the streets of Milan with despair in her heart but provokes lust in the mind of every man who turns to look at her. It is a perfect cin-ematic moment of alienation.

Equally vivid in my memory is Dilys Powell's confidence in Luis Buñuel's *Viridiana* (1961). The scene in which Silvia Pinal's nun was raped by a gang of beggars to the refrain of Handel's 'Hallelujah Chorus' led to the film being banned in the director's own country, which was still under the rule of Franco and the Fascist Party. Today it still arouses the wrath of Mrs Whitehouse and her supporters whenever it is shown on television. Yet in the 1960s Dilys Powell gave a robust defence of the film's morality to the readers of the *Sunday Times*. *Viridiana*, she was able to explain, was an attack on religious hypocrisy. Charity and concern are not always the most effective ways of dealing with the under-class. The poor and desperate may find a very different means of unleashing their frustration on the privileged. The same Dilys Powell was to write about Dirk Bogarde's performance as the com-poser in Visconti's *Death in Venice* (1971) as the cinematic equiva-lent of watching an old friend dying. George Melly in the *Observer* stressed the same theme about the film: a well-loved English actor being taken on a gondola towards the very heart of darkness while engulfed by the most extraordinary light.

In similar ways these critics championed the arrival of Louis Malle, Jean Luc Godard and in particular François Truffaut. His *Jules et Jim* (1962) was hailed as the most triumphant cinematic celebration of a novel yet seen. Nuances of character, background and narrative had finally been captured on celluloid in a manner that made the reading of the original novel on which it was based almost redundant. Film criticism was firmly linked to a humanistic tradition in which the individual artist was able to hold on to the reins. No critic would have the same confidence today. If a similar row occurred about Buñuel's *Viridiana* in the Sunday newspapers in the mid-1990s, a whole host of opinions would be canvassed other than those of the leading film critic. We would be subjected

to endless think pieces about blasphemy in the arts. Leading
Spanish residents in Britain, including possibly Michael Portillo,
would be reined in to give a critical thumbs down to Buñuel and
all that he stood for. *The Late Show* review panel would undoubtedly congratulate the Spanish director on appealing to the lowest
common denominator in the audience, but would suggest that his
narrative technique might benefit from spending time with the
more streetwise auteurs of Hollywood.

The *Observer*'s current film critic Philip French ought to be
included in the pantheon of talent described above. French has an
intelligence, knowledge of cinema and commitment to the medium
that is certainly the equal of a George Melly, Penelope Gilliat or
Dilys Powell. Yet he differs from his predecessors in one crucial
aspect. His only frame of moral reference comes from other
movies. The first paragraph of a Philip French review is almost
invariably a reference list. He can only write about a film after
relating it to other notable films in the same genre. In this he
reflects a genuine change in the practice of both film-making and
criticism over the past decade. Nearly every Hollywood movie
today refers to some other movie. Whether a romantic comedy like
Sleepless in Seattle, a cartoon like *The Lion King* or a thriller like
Seven, contemporary Hollywood movies steal plots and subject
matter from other movies. *Seattle* becomes a remake of *An Affair
to Remember*, *The Lion King* a revisiting of *Bambi*, while the bar-
barities of *Seven* are excused by visual references to countless
1940s film noirs. It was the French New Wave that began the
trend. Truffaut and Jean Luc Godard borrowed ruthlessly and
sometimes ironically from Hollywood pulp thrillers and
romances. The films would often include visual tributes to the
movies on which they were based. Arthur Penn's *Bonnie and
Clyde* (1967) and Peter Bogdanovich's *The Last Picture Show*
(1971) took over the tradition. A decade later the dominant
Hollywood movies were Steven Spielberg's *Indiana Jones* cycle
and George Lucas's evolving *Star Wars* trilogy. Referring to a host
of previous cliff-hanging serials and films – from *Flash Gordon* to
Sexton Blake – the adventures appealed to a cinema-literate public

that was being entertained in a naïve and sophisticated manner at the same time.

While the process may have enriched the cinema, it has undoubtedly led to more tedious and pretentious film criticism. The majority of Philip French's fellow critics now follow his line, and judgements are formed only with reference to other movies. Thus the excesses of Tarantino's followers – directors who are making more violent and bloody films than *Reservoir Dogs* or *Pulp Fiction* – are described by the critics as homages to an original master. No moral view is taken of their meaning or influence. No concern is expressed about the lack of originality in the majority of new screenplays because the critics are not looking for new material in the first place. The great European directors are long gone. So, like the producers who pitch high-concept movies to studio heads, our new film reviewers adore the old models.

The one director whose reputation remains unassailable to both film-makers and critics is Alfred Hitchcock. His *Psycho* in particular has been the inspiration behind a plethora of critically acclaimed yet dubious Hollywood thrillers of the past twenty years. One of the few British directors to have done his best work in Hollywood, Hitchcock took total control over a whole production: from supervising the screenplay to storyboarding each and every moment of the drama before commencing filming. Brian de Palma is only the first in a long line of Hollywood directors who have paid homage to the master through a cycle of films about serial killers. De Palma's *Obsession* (1976) and *Dressed to Kill* (1980) are reworkings of Hitchcock's *Vertigo* and *Psycho*. The director of course denies that he has been influenced by Hitchcock. According to his film biography on the Microsoft 1995 Cinemania CD-ROM, de Palma responds to criticism that he is portraying graphic violence by the fact that 'he is incorporating Eisenstein's theory of montage as conflict, that "film is violence"'.

An observation like that – pretentious and inaccurate – could easily crop up in a film review today, especially in the broadsheets. Yet in his own time Hitchcock was the subject of considerable controversy. The critics were worried by the amorality of *Psycho*. Saul

Bellow in his novel *More Die of Heartbreak* uses *Psycho* as a key reference to a turning point in American culture. In the novel a respected teacher falls in love with a younger woman named Matilda. A trip to watch Hitchcock's *Psycho* marks the beginning of a change in their relationship. The fact that Matilda loves the movie is a sign of her amorality and essential stupidity. There are even moments when she begins to resemble the psychopath in the film. The teacher knows he should not marry her. He has seen *Psycho* before and a second viewing does not change his mind about its essential wickedness: 'I hated it. I hate all that excitement without a focus. Nothing but conditional reflexes they've trained you into. That's what stands out in the video films I've been watching . . . They keep you uneasy and give you one murder after another. You presently stop asking, Why are they killing this guy?'

There cannot be a great deal of doubt that Hitchcock used murder for cinematic effect in *Psycho* rather than for any moral truth. Yet he is the one director that both Hollywood and Europe now regard as sacrosanct. *Psycho* remains the most influential Hollywood film of the past thirty years. It took a peanut of psychological truth and thereby justified the breaking of a thousand taboos. But Hitchcock did not indulge in graphic violence as a film-maker. He was interested in suspense, the suggestion of violence off-screen. In *Psycho* the notorious shower scene takes up a minimal amount of screen time. Hitchcock never shows the knife in actual contact with Janet Leigh's body. The director literally cuts away to our imaginations before any physical action occurs. Yet cinema critics today will justify any amount of graphic violence on the screen by referring directly to Hitchcock's *Psycho*. At the end of Danny Boyle's *Shallow Grave* the heroine plunges a dagger deep into the shoulder of a boyfriend she no longer trusts. We see and hear the knife crashing through bone and skin to the floorboard beneath the body. Nothing is left to the imagination. The critics hailed the moment as a truly Hitchcockian sequence. But it wasn't; the old master would have constructed the scene in a completely different way. When in doubt the new generation of film critics refer to Hitchcock – and increasingly Tarantino – in order to avoid making a moral judgement about a film. Perhaps it no longer matters. At a time when the majority of Hollywood movies attempt to outdo one another in their self-referential depiction of graphic violence, does anyone really care that the critics can no longer tell the dancer from the dance?

6 Epilogue

The collapse of morale in public broadcasting and the struggle for
survival in our theatres has partly come about because of a political reaction against the liberal values of the 1960s. Politicians have
spent a great deal of effort over the past fifteen years persuading us
to take careers in business more seriously. Newspapers have given
over a huge amount of space to the same cause, denouncing a per-
missive culture of thirty years ago that seemed to turn us all into
poets or rock musicians. Yet the fact remains that, if other coun-
tries envy us at all, it is for our ability to make good television programmes rather than reliable motor cars. The new plays on our
stages and the films we back have become an important part of
our national identity – something we've actually been good at. It is
ironic that, at a time when much of this identity is under threat,
our colleges and universities are packed with a generation of students learning about film, television and theatre. There are literally
thousands of students attending media courses that are supposedly
preparing them for careers in the entertainment industry. Like any
generation, they have hopes and dreams that are likely to remain
unfulfilled. Out of the thousands who are determined to direct
their own films, only a handful will succeed. Yet they are seeking
to join a profession under conditions that would have been
unthinkable to a previous generation. The traditional entry points
– a traineeship with the BBC or an assistant director post at a
thriving regional theatre – have all but disappeared. More than
half the workforce of the ITV companies have been made redundant or turned freelance over the past fifteen years. The BBC has
turned itself into a vast internal market place whose production

base now competes for product almost under the same terms as a car manufacturer. Aspiring young actors can no longer rely on local-authority grants to assist them at drama schools. The young are facing a new and ruthlessly competitive environment in which to develop their talents.

It is perhaps unsurprising that they should sometimes look back to the 1960s with wonder and a little jealousy. Their own pop idols can't quite compete in fame or fortune with the Beatles or Bob Dylan. Writers do not have access to the hundreds of hours that were given over to the single play on primetime television in those days. If our theatres are experiencing a new golden age, it is in a strangely muted colour compared to the ten years in which the Royal Court, the National and the Royal Shakespeare Company first flourished. Does any of this really matter? Is this another lament for a supposed lost paradise that in reality never existed? After all, the clock cannot be turned back. Tom Stoppard has argued that it is pointless to sit around regretting the passing of the days in the 1960s when he and his friends saw every new production at the Bristol Old Vic. Times change. Modern teenagers might get equal satisfaction out of staying up all night surfing the Internet. Is there really any difference? I believe there is. The way any society treats its talent is an indicator of both its health and generosity. There is and has to be a context for creativity – a process of patronage – without which even the most gifted can go to the wall.

The writers I have most closely observed in this book – David Hare, Alan Bleasdale, Dennis Potter and Mike Leigh – have all benefited from the long-term patronage of a theatre or broadcaster. The body of work they now represent would not have existed without that patronage; but it also could not have come about without the sheer single-mindedness of the writers themselves. In *A Dance to the Music of Time*, the novelist Anthony Powell describes the presence of talent in his generation as at once its most vulnerable and yet most robust characteristic. Given the right circumstances, the writer can become the most bloody-minded of survivors. It was the Royal Court in the 1950s that first gave playwrights a chance to be at the centre of the dramatic process. Here

was a theatre in which acting, direction and lighting were all sub-
servient to the intentions of the script. A generation of directors –
Tony Richardson, Lindsay Anderson, William Gaskill and John
Dexter – all took their first inspiration from the text. Nuance, texture, meaning and a fundamental simplicity (by no means simple
to achieve) became the primary objectives in the staging of any
new play. This did not mean that the directors were minor figures.
Dexter ran his productions with a military precision, often instill-
ing fear and trembling into the actors and writer until his highest
ambitions were achieved. Anderson and Gaskill were notorious
for their waspish sensibilities and dominant personalities. Yet their
talents were primarily given over to the interpretation of a text.
The influence of this work spread way beyond the Royal ·Court's
smallish theatre in Sloane Square. It won a worldwide reputation
for the theatre's writers and actors as well as the directors. It
opened the door for a generation of television directors to work on
scripts in a similar way, particularly on the BBC's *Play for Today*
strand in the 1960s and 1970s. It probably led to the most creative
period in English theatre since the Jacobeans. The Royal Court
writers of the 1950s and 1960s did not think of themselves as
fringe playwrights. They were running the revolution.

During the 1980s American playwrights like David Mamet,
Tony Kushner, Wallace Shawn and even Arthur Miller had their
work premièred in London – although by no means exclusively in
Sloane Square – rather than on Broadway because of their admiration for the kind of writers' theatre pioneered by the Court. At the
Royal Court itself Max Stafford-Clark's championing of Caryl
Churchill was one of the few strong writer–director partnerships
to emerge. The new generation of British directors have tended to
favour classic revivals over new work, and this did have an effect
on the Court's output and identity. It is perhaps why so many of its
writers in the 1980s failed to fulfil their promise. Writers need the
best directors for their work to develop and flourish. The plays of
Sarah Daniels and Louise Page were often presented in an *ad hoc*
and comparatively low-key way. Unlike their male counterparts,
these writers did not bang the table and ask for better. It remains

to be seen whether Stephen Daldry's legacy at the Royal Court will encourage a new generation of directors to give priority to new work rather than to classic revivals or their own film careers.

In television the disenfranchisement of writers has been even more decisive. Producers at the BBC and ITV are no longer able to provide any kind of continuity or long-term commitment to talent. Due to fear of competition from satellite and cable, the BBC and ITV are engaged in a ratings war whereby the success of a show is judged on whether it is watched by an audience of 10 million. A writer is therefore only as good as his or her last performance in the ratings. As a consequence, BBC1 and ITV now only commission formula drama. If it isn't a cop show, medical drama or classic adaptation, it simply won't be produced. The tradition of television drama as represented by David Mercer and Dennis Potter, *Edge of Darkness* or *The Boys From the Blackstuff* has all but been abandoned. Yet there is no evidence that this is something the viewers asked for. The executive fear that has brought about the dismantling of television drama is entirely self-generated. Even today the viewing of satellite and cable counts for less than 10 per cent of the audience. People want to see original drama on the mainstream channels – which is in any case something satellite doesn't provide. There is of course nothing intrinsically wrong with formula drama. Some of the strongest television drama in recent years has come from police series like *Prime Suspect* and *Cracker*. But there is something wrong if it is the *only* kind of drama that television is offering. It means that the BBC and ITV are lowering the expectations of audiences where once they raised them. If people are only watching the instantly familiar, the easiest genres – whether cop or costume – it means they will lose patience with anything else. The kind of challenging drama that can appeal to viewers on different levels, once pioneered by the BBC, is on the verge of extinction. In some ways it makes life easier for everyone. Television executives are no longer dogged by controversial plays. Viewers can regard television drama as pure escapism. The critics can continue their campaign to report on television as complete trivia. As Wallace Shawn revealed in *The Designated Mourner*, becoming lowbrow can be fun.

Meanwhile broadcasters, with Channel 4 in the vanguard, are encouraging writers to think screenplay. Writing movies is the one bright new star left in the constellation. Everyone wants a piece of LA culture – if not literally, then by way of the word processor. Yet a career as a writer in Hollywood means rarely being able to see a script through from the first idea to final production. The majority of screenplays pass through several writing hands before being given the green light. If a prestigious director becomes involved, the script will undoubtedly be rewritten again. If a star name is on board – and in most cases they have to be – he or she will have a huge input into the development process. Directors, producers, stars and their agents rule in Hollywood, not the writer. We are, of course, a long way from this situation in Britain. But even on comparatively low-budget features, often financed by either Channel 4 or the BBC, it is the director and producer who are at the creative helm.

It is worth remembering that the majority of feature films for television are being produced by the independent sector. It was the birth of Channel 4 in 1982 that gave the first real encouragement to independent production in Britain. Before Channel 4, all television drama and film was produced in-house at either the BBC or ITV by creative teams employed on long-term contracts. Jeremy Isaacs, Channel 4's first chief executive, always saw the work of independent producers as complementary to that of the BBC and ITV's in-house staff. Yet he suspected that independent producers might bring a freshness and flexibility to television that often eluded the rival channels. Independent producers were meant to have an independence of mind and spirit in their choice of project. In this the new channel proved to be an unqualified success, not least in its feature-film policy. ITV and the BBC began shedding permanent staff in favour of independent producers. The government decreed that 25 per cent of all production from the BBC and ITV should be handed over to the independent sector. The independents themselves began to emerge as the self-proclaimed leaders of a brave new market place. Business plans, market share and profitability became the talk of the town, at least at the Groucho Club in Soho.

As the commissioning editor for drama at Channel 4, I was able to observe this sea-change among independent producers. They would no longer arrive in my office with a writer whose idea for a project would then be discussed. Now they turned up writer-less but with a high concept in tow. There would be much talk of front- and back-end deals that meant little or nothing to me. They would express great admiration for the channel, although further investigation would reveal that they had managed to see very little of its actual output. Finally it emerged that their high concept was little more than a common-or-garden detective story, but to be written and shot 'in a completely new way' – which always turned out to be the shooting style of the no-longer-new *NYPD Blue*. They had everything to bring to the table, except a writer. The project – I would then be told – lent itself brilliantly to the American concept of team-writing. Could I recommend any names?

I never did, of course, because they had – to use a term beloved by independent producers – made a bad pitch. No American producer would ever pitch to a Network executive in this style. The latter would only be interested in the quality of the idea and the talent being brought to the station. The truth is that the majority of independent producers in this country have no access whatsoever to the best dramatic talent. They are running businesses and, unlike their one-time counterparts at the BBC or ITV, lack budgets and motivation to commission scripts or form creative partnerships with writers. In response, I began to empower writers by making them executive producers: Alan Bleasdale on *GBH*, Dennis Potter on *Lipstick On Your Collar*, Hugh Whitemore on *A Dance to the Music of Time* (1997) and, though she did not take an actual credit, Paula Milne on *The Politician's Wife* (1995) and *The Fragile Heart* (1996). This led to a sense of outrage among other producers and, more surprisingly, the press. Empowering writers meant indulging them, I was told. The writer-as-producer would never change a line of dialogue or be prepared to cut a single scene from a film. Even though some of the most loved American shows (*NYPD Blue*, for instance, or *Frasier*) have their leading writers as executive producers, this country firmly believes that writers should be kept as far away from the production process as possible.

Yet empowering a writer was precisely the key to the success of the Royal Court in 1956. In that theatre writers worked alongside the director through script discussions, casting, rehearsal and the final dress run. The most talented writers are the least defensive about their work and will accept suggestions for cuts and changes in a script when they are presented in an intelligent and coherent way. Bleasdale, for instance, cut eighty pages out of the first draft of *GBH*. But writers also have an awkward habit of saying no when they feel that the central vision of a piece is being threatened. Then they are prepared to fight, argue, chew the carpet and even go down on their knees and beg to retain a line that is important to them. This working method leads to drama in which the voice of the writer still counts. It is a comment on our times and culture that we are beginning to fear it.

Mentioning the Royal Court in 1956 recalls the title of its most famous play: *Look Back in Anger*. The writers analysed in this book often conceived their work in anger, as a kind of controlled rage against authority and the powers that be which their critics mistakenly dismiss as old-fashionedly left wing. Yet Hare, Bleasdale, Potter and Leigh took for granted the fact that they could be in opposition to the institutions for which they worked. The assumption that art is anger – that it is in opposition – appears to be far more problematic today. It exists hardly anywhere within the media. The younger writers and directors who pass through my office do not appear to be particularly angry. In fact they are all too eager to please – both audiences and the broadcaster. But then no one is asking the young to be angry. Even seemingly controversial work, like *Mojo* or *Trainspotting*, appeals to a targeted young audience who share the writers' and directors' relish for Tarantino and the drug culture. As plays and films, they are not at heart truly challenging. Some would argue that this speaks for a fundamental change in the taste of the audience. But I can only see it as a failure of nerve by many of those who are in charge of our theatre and television companies. For it is Los Angeles rather than Liverpool which rules most of their thinking today.

Index